Your Road Map to Retirement

Your Road Map to Retirement

◆

Solutions When You're Lost

Brett DeFore
Registered Investment Advisor

iUniverse, Inc.
New York Lincoln Shanghai

Your Road Map to Retirement
Solutions When You're Lost

Copyright © 2007 by Brett DeFore

All rights reserved. No part of this book may be used or reproduced by any means, graphic, electronic, or mechanical, including photocopying, recording, taping or by any information storage retrieval system without the written permission of the publisher except in the case of brief quotations embodied in critical articles and reviews.

iUniverse books may be ordered through booksellers or by contacting:

iUniverse
2021 Pine Lake Road, Suite 100
Lincoln, NE 68512
www.iuniverse.com
1-800-Authors (1-800-288-4677)

Because of the dynamic nature of the Internet, any Web addresses or links contained in this book may have changed since publication and may no longer be valid.

The views expressed in this work are solely those of the author and do not necessarily reflect the views of the publisher, and the publisher hereby disclaims any responsibility for them.

ISBN: 978-0-595-45538-6 (pbk)
ISBN: 978-0-595-69520-1 (cloth)
ISBN: 978-0-595-89847-3 (ebk)

Printed in the United States of America

Contents

Introduction		vii
CHAPTER 1	Where Do I Start?	1
CHAPTER 2	Dreams: Planning: Goals	9
CHAPTER 3	Driving Without a Road Map	12
CHAPTER 4	Practice Retirement First	21
CHAPTER 5	How Much Income Will I Need in Retirement?	26
CHAPTER 6	Finding More Income	34
CHAPTER 7	Getting the Most from Social Security, Medicare, and Medigap	47
CHAPTER 8	Allocating Assets in Retirement	60
CHAPTER 9	Get in Touch with your Emotions	66
CHAPTER 10	Obstacles to Avoid	75
CHAPTER 11	Can I Do it Alone?	86
CHAPTER 12	Stay Organized	104
CHAPTER 13	Beating the Markets	111
CHAPTER 14	Buy a Ladder for Income	120
CHAPTER 15	Annuities in Retirement	127
CHAPTER 16	Retirement Plan and IRA Distribution Issues	143
CHAPTER 17	Do I Really Need Insurance?	150
CHAPTER 18	Planning Your Estate	165

Chapter 19	Giving 180
Chapter 20	Preparing the Next Generation of Retirees 191

Conclusion 193

Appendix A 195

Introduction

Ask a mountain climber their ultimate dream climb and they may respond, "Everest". Each climber may have a specific reason as to why Everest would be their dream climb, but for many Everest represents the pinnacle of all climbs.

Many see Everest as an opportunity to rest on one of its summits and to say, 'they've been close to God'. In the past hundred years, thousands of individuals have made the attempt to reach one of Everest's summits but only two thousand four hundred climbers have actually attained the goal. While these ascensions have been documented and celebrated, What is lost are the nearly two hundred climbers who have lost their lives climbing to fulfill a dream.

What many people fail to realize are the odds of surviving Everest are only one in eight, let alone reaching the summit. Some may think it's within reason that only two hundred people have lost their lives while attempting to climb Everest, but what people may not know is that more than twenty percent of these deaths have occurred during the descent from the summit. Whether it was to carelessness, lack of focus, or simply taking the mountain for granted, the point is a high percentage of casualties have occurred at some of the least suspecting times.

Climbers, especially those individuals who tackle landmarks like such as a Mt. Everest, will tell you that preparation is a key for success. Preparation includes areas such as the health of the individual, experience, equipment, determination, financial resources and time. It requires a guide who has the experience to lead you up the mountain towards the summit. It's more than simply strapping on your hiking boots and climbing a mountain.

Today Baby Boomers are beginning their ascension into retirement. Like climbers, Boomers who have properly prepared themselves for the task at hand, may have an opportunity to realize a successful ascent as it relates to the dreams and goals they've envisioned for themselves in retirement, but unfortunately many have started the climb without the proper equipment or adequate financial resources.

According to U.S. Census data, it is estimated that nearly ten thousand future retirees will turn 60 every day for the next seventeen years. This type of information should be good news for businesses that cater to retirees, but the world of retirement could be a harsh place for a retiree if he isn't prepared for the elements.

If you're like most Boomers who are in or at the verge of retirement, it's likely you've had some sleepless nights wondering about the future and asking questions such as; Can I afford to retire? How do I take care of my parents? Do I want to continue working until I qualify for Medicare? What am I going to do after I retire? Do I have enough assets to outlive me and my wife? You've spent the better part of forty years working towards this day, but now that it's finally near, all you have are more questions.

As humans we spend our lives saving and scratching for one major goal after another. First it was a house, then kids, then college, then helping our kids, helping our parents, and now helping ourselves to build a nest egg. We daydreamed about the future and looked forward to the day when we could leave the work force and sail off into *Retirement Land,* but now that it's finally here, we realize that while they may have left one job, we have just been assigned a new one that could last a long time, Vice President of Nest Egg Inc.

As you approach or enter retirement the sooner you realize that you are responsible for securing your own retirement, the more prepared you will be to handle life's elements. Retirement is a journey that requires careful preparation and planning. Just because you've reached the summit, doesn't mean you can let your guard down. You have to constantly monitor your progression in order to avoid the pitfalls that could face you in retirement.

Climbers are prepared for the terrain of Everest, but weather is unpredictable. In retirement you may have an idea as to the direction you want to travel, but unforeseen events could force you to make changes to your plan. What will be important is how you react to these events.

Life in retirement will be affected by change. These changes could come from government, health, family, work, or another unforeseen event. When these changes occur, and they will occur, it's important that you have a contingency plan in place to limit damage that may occur to you and your family. Most of the deaths that occurred on Everest were due to poor planning, carelessness, and the lack of a contingency plan. For the remaining two thousand climbers, their preparation offered them the ability to reach the summit and to see their families once again.

For more than twenty years I have had the opportunity to serve as a guide to investors and retirees as they ascend toward their financial summit. For some it's been college education, for others, it's having enough income to afford the retirement they've always wanted. My experience helped me guide these investors on the best path based upon their needs and goals. Some paths were more treacherous while others took a bit longer, but each route was created based upon their specific dreams and goals.

If you are serious about your retirement, take this opportunity to plan for your journey. Your journey will require all of your senses to be sharp. Just as Everest is the biggest climb for mountain climbers, retirement will be your last summit.

This book was written to serve as a handbook during retirement. Rely on this book to tackle the elements you will face during retirement. The following chapters will provide answers to the many questions you may have about retirement. Use this information to educate yourself on the potential obstacles you will face in retirement and to select a retirement route which is the best route suited for you and your family.

1

Where Do I Start?

Concerned, confused, anxious, scared, these are just a few of the emotions that you're likely facing today if you are retired or nearing retirement.

It's likely you've held the same job, followed the same schedule, and had the same hobbies and interest for more than thirty years. Suddenly you find yourself with time on your hands, no work responsibilities, no schedule, and no paycheck. It's only normal that you have questions and concerns, but before you let your emotions get the best of you, let's talk about what's really changed since you've officially announced you're retired or about to retire.

Even though you find yourself retired or close to retirement, it's important that *you* take control of your retirement and not allow your emotions to take control of you. Retirement is just another time in your life that has importance. During our everyday lives, we missed out on the little things that occurred everyday, but we remember the life changing events that had an impact in our lives such as marriage, the purchase of the first house, a new baby, a new job, and paying for college. All of these events created different emotions but eventually you gathered information and confidence and proceeded on with your life. Retirement will be another life changing event.

If you took heed of advice given to you many years ago when retirement plans were available and lived within your means, you may be an individual who will actually enjoy retirement. You can pretty much skip this chapter and move on to some other chapters that may be of more benefit, but if you're one of those individuals who worked until the last day and hasn't really planned for the future, or aren't sure whether you can move forward into retirement, hopefully the remaining chapters will provide information you can use as you enjoy your retirement years.

Planning for retirement should be taken very seriously. The years you spent waiting up for your son or daughter to get home every night while they were in high school or college may pale in comparison to the sleepless nights you may have worrying about your future if you aren't prepared and have answers to your questions. If you haven't started any type of planning, it's time to start, so let's begin.

1. Have a Plan

Remember a time when you were driving on a road and had absolutely no idea where you were? It's not a comfortable feeling is it? You likely felt helpless until you took the time to ask for help, retrace your steps or consult a map. Would you ever consider getting in your car and driving to New York City without a roadmap? Sure, you may have an idea as to the direction you want to go, but how long would it take? How many people would you need to talk to along the way? How many mistakes would you make before you reached your final destination? What would it cost?

Unfortunately many Americans may not have taken the time to plan for children, college, or career changes, planning for retirement is something you need to take very seriously. Especially in today's environment where a fifty year old worker is considered to be too expensive for companies and pension plans are a thing of the past, planning for retirement is crucial.

There are various ways you can actually plan for retirement, but plans should start at the same spot which is identifying the dreams you may have. Retirement is another stage in your life similar to other stages you've completed, but it's the last stage in your life and it requires your full attention.

You may have received information from your company, talked with friends and family members, or read books or magazines that provided some insight as to what you can expect your retirement life to look like. While this information is helpful, you will need specific answers to questions such as, can you afford to retire? What will your expenses be? Should you continue to delay Social Security payments? When should you pull assets from my IRA? Where will you live? In essence, you need a thorough examination of where you are today, and a written plan that will help guide you through the various stages of retirement.

As you prepare your plan, understand that it's impossible to precisely map out your retirement and have everything fall into place according to the plan. Your plan will be a work in progress as outside forces attack your dreams. Retirement is an evolution just like a long road trip. It is constantly changing based upon the conditions that are present. When these conditions change, it's important that you have a plan of action that can get you back on course, or select another route that serves the best interest of you and your family. The planning you do today could not only avoid obstacles in the future, but provide you with the confidence in knowing that your retirement dreams can be attained.

2. Income

Income is the life source to your retirement dreams and goals. Just as antibiotics play an essential role in our life, income can cure many ills that attack our retirement future. The amount of income you have coming into the household could determine everything from where you will live, what you can afford to eat, where you will eat, travel, family, prescriptions, and insurance coverage. If you don't know what the income flow is into the household, then DON'T SPEND ANOTHER DIME until you know.

Several experts have opinions as to the amount of income you will need during your retirement years. The most accurate gauge is to consider your income prior to retirement. It's likely during these years you were working, your income was relatively stable, and thus you became accustomed to that standard of living.

You may have read opinions which suggest retirees may need as much as 70 percent of pre-retirement income to maintain the lifestyle to which you've become accustomed. It is estimated that if you do not have a pension, or other liquid assets, Social Security may only provide 40 percent of your pre-retirement income, which means, if you haven't planned for your future, you may need to find another 30 percent, or dramatically cut back on your lifestyle.

If you're one of the lucky ones who worked for a company for several years and are receiving a pension or contributed to your 401(k) or IRA's, you are far ahead of other retirees today who are hoping that Social Security will be around to fund their needs, but a recent study completed by the Employee Benefit Research Institute in 2007 points out that only 33 percent of workers over the age of 55 have at least $250,000 available in liquid assets to generate income for their retirement. Assuming a retiree is able to generate a 5 percent return on those assets, it means an additional $12,500 per year in interest.

This income will help in the short term, but a problem most people fail to realize is the future cost of living. Just because your retired doesn't meant that prices of goods and services stay the same, in fact in many cases the cost to retirees actually increase when you consider travel costs, prescription and medical costs. These inflationary costs have historically averaged more than five percent over the past decade which means, over the next five years this income may not be enough to cover your living expenses and you may need to dip into principle in order to cover basic needs such as food, healthcare, and utilities, a thought that many retirees don't want to consider.

Finding additional income could have a great impact on your retirement future which is why an entire chapter is dedicated to the various things you could consider to maximize the income.

3. Expenses

If income is the penicillin to many ills, expenses are the disease. Several financial experts have tried to share knowledge as to how you can gauge your expenses in retirement as it relates to a percentage of your income. In reality you could spend more money shortly after you've retired simply due to the free time you have. Free time means you can spend more time traveling, fixing up the house, reading, entertainment, and new hobbies. All of these activities typically require money. There's nothing wrong with activities. They are short term in nature and will usually dissipate over time. Just make sure you understand the difference between a normal budgetary expense that will come up every month such as utilities, insurance, food, house maintenance and what are one time events or off balance sheet items such as restorations, travel, charities, or hobbies.

Income is easier to estimate. Expenses tend to be more of a moving target. A recommended strategy would be to invest in a software program such as Quicken or Microsoft Money which allows you to monitor your expenses. If you can actually see where you are spending your money, you may change your habits in such a way to cut your expenses or increase your income.

If you don't have access to a computer or these programs, AARP is a great resource (www.aarp.org) which provides sheets where you can record your income and expenses on paper. They list many of the items you may take for granted as you evaluate your household expenses. You can visit your local library and download this information from the internet or contact AARP and they will send them to you directly.

An important step to consider as you anticipate your monthly expenses is to be sure you take the time to create an emergency or "just in case". This type of fund is designed to cover those unexpected issues that could impact your household budget when you least expect it. Issues such as an heat and air system going bad, a hole in the roof, unforeseen medical expenses, unemployment, repairs on a family car, or assistance with a family member. These types of funds should be liquid assets that are readily available and are not subject to market fluctuations. This doesn't mean you need to have these assets sit in cash or savings accounts. You could consider having them invested in short term c.d.'s, money market accounts, limited duration income mutual funds, or other short term investments that be gotten to easily.

Many financial experts suggest you should set aside a total amount that equates to three to six months of your budgeted monthly expenses. If you don't have the funds available today, make contributions to an account over time, and add it as an expense to your budget until the proper amount is reached. We never know what life events may occur in the future, thus it's best to have a fund set up for these emergencies. Try to fill this fund as quickly as possible so that when one of life's emergency comes calling, you'll be prepared.

4. Review Insurance Policies

This is a great time to review the insurance coverage on many of your assets such as your home, cars, life, and health coverage. Depending on your condition, you may find that you no longer require life or disability insurance, so the funds you were using to help pay for disability could be used to purchase Medigap replacement or long term care.

AARP recently surveyed forty-five year olds about several topics. One of these topics dealt with insurance related costs during retirement. When these soon to be retirees were asked about long term care, nearly 50 percent of the respondents said they were worried about long term care costs in the future, but only 18 percent actually considered buying insurance. Many seniors make the mistake in assuming that their assisted living needs could be paid for by Medicare and Medicaid should they need nursing home assistance. This is only true after most of your assets have been used to fund nursing home care.

According to AARP, the average stay is over two and a half years and could cost as much as $71,000 per year. The U.S. Census Bureau points out that by 2010, nearly half of the population will be caring for an elderly parent, and over 30 percent of these individuals will have a stroke and likely need long term care themselves. Those whole life and universal life insurance policies may be more valuable by owning a long term care policy that offers you care when you need it.

Once again we a full chapter is dedicated to discussing the issue of insurance and the types of policies you may need.

5. Social Security and Medicare

About three months prior to the month of your 65th birthday, or three months before you wish to start collecting benefits, you should apply for Social Security. As of 2006 you may apply as early as 62.8 years of age, but benefits are reduced, depending on your full retirement age (determined by your year of birth). Applying early can reduce your benefit by 20 percent or more, but the timing of taking the benefit depends on your circumstances.

If your family has a healthy history, or you are comfortable with your current income, you may choose to delay your benefit in order to receive your full benefit at age 70 according to current Federal guidelines. Make sure you check Federal guidelines before you sign up for Social Security. Full benefits are likely to change for retirees as we continue to live longer lives. If you're sick or have a questionable family health history, or need the income now, it may make sense to take the benefit as soon as possible.

Along with Social Security, one of the benefits of being a retiree is the availability of Medicare. Medicare is our country's health insurance program for people age 65 or older. Certain people younger than age 65 can qualify for Medicare, too, including those who have disabilities and those who have permanent kidney failure or amyotrophic lateral sclerosis (Lou Gehrig's disease). The program helps with the cost of health care, but it does not cover all medical expenses or the cost of most long-term care.

As the law stands today, Medicare has four major components which effect retirees over age sixty-five, they are:

- Hospital Insurance: Part A is the portion helps pay for inpatient care in the hospital or skilled nursing facility (following a hospital stay), some home health care and hospice care.
- Medical Insurance: Part B helps pay for doctor services and many other medical services and supplies that are not covered under Part A.
- Medical Advantage Insurance: Part C formerly known as Medicare and Choice plans is available in many areas. People with Medicare Parts A and B can choose to receive all their health care services through one of the provider organizations listed under Part C.
- Prescription Drug Insurance: Part D helps pay for medications that doctors prescribe for treatment.

The Centers for Medicare & Medicaid Services is the agency in charge of the Medicare program. But you apply for Medicare at Social Security by visiting their website at www.medicare.gov or contacting them via a toll free number at 1-800-MEDICARE.

6. Simplify Your Life

Many retirees have learned lessons from their parents that it's not in your best interest to have everything in one place. These were lessons from another time when investors were not protected by the government or other forms of insurance. Today, we are finding that there is strength in numbers. Several financial institutions offer lower fees, higher interest, and better loan rates if you reach specific asset levels or loan amounts. While this may not be an incentive to some, the idea of working with one institution that has a complete understanding of your needs and goals may be in your best interest.

Many banks and investment firms today offer services that are free to their clients such as check writing, bill pay services, and investment services. Market turmoil over the past decade has forced many firms to concentrate on financial and retirement planning for their clients. Today many investment firms offer outstanding planning and investment advice for retirees.

These firms can help you during retirement by providing a financial professional who understands your needs, goals, and tolerance for risk as it relates to your investments. These professionals tend to be more patient and offer a higher degree of communication with their clients, especially during more tumultuous conditions. The professional who helps you monitor your retirement assets could not only simplify your life by having someone oversee your investments, but save you TIME and MONEY and ultimately help you reach and maintain you retirement dreams.

More information is provided to help you find the right institution and person to help you manage your investments during retirement in Chapter 11 Can I Manage My Nest Egg Alone?

7. Estate Planning

It's likely you've been so busy since you've decided to retire that the last thing you've considered is the effectiveness of your current will. Everyone should have a will, but a will alone may not be enough to protect your assets and help reduce estate taxes and other costs.

In these complicated times you may want to consider other options that protect taxes against your estate. This is a perfect time to sit down with your lawyer to review your will, trust, powers of attorney, beneficiary designations, and investment plans to make sure that you and your beneficiaries are appropriately protected. If you do not have a will or attorney, consult with a friend or financial professional, and have them arrange an interview opportunity for you. A full chapter on Estate Planning is dedicated in this book.

As you begin your retirement journey, these are just a few of the major issues you need to plan for. Not everyone starts at the same place and time, but all of these issues may play a vital role in your future. It's important to take the time and understand how each one of these major areas could affect your family so you are prepared in your retirement years.

2

Dreams: Planning: Goals

It was the morning of October 10, 2005, and I did something that I hadn't done in nearly eighteen years. I stepped on the scale in my bathroom. I don't know why I had chosen this particular morning; I just know that when I waited for the digital number to come up, it was a lot more than what I had ever imagined. The number was more than 300 pounds!

I had never really thought about my weight all that often. I knew that I was what they considered a "big man", but I never really worried about just how big. I was an person who played golf, tennis from time to time, and still visited the workout room, but over the eighteen years of marriage I had seen my waist size climb from a smelt thirty four inch waist to a husky forty two. I wasn't happy about the way I looked. I knew what I used to look like and dreamed of getting there again, but I would likely need some help.

I hired a personal trainer who completed a thorough exam of my abilities. He asked me what I hoped to accomplish and where I wanted to be. In essence, he wanted to know my *dreams*.

Once he understood the dreams I had for myself, he took measurements of my body, asked me about my diet, the types of exercises I had been doing, the amount of time I exercised weekly, how long each time, and areas that I wanted to concentrate on. Once he gathered this information, he provided me with a *plan* to follow.

The plan would be monitored over the coming weeks and *goals* would be established. Initially the goals were very small such as increasing the number of minutes on the treadmill, the amount of weight being used for each exercise or the number of repetitions. As weeks turned into months measurements were taken of my body to determine where other changes had occurred. As goals were being surpassed, new goals were being created.

The journey that I began in October 2005 would not be a smooth one. The first few weeks started off very well as I lost about fifteen pounds and two inches off my waste relatively quickly, but I didn't continue my work. It wasn't until a photo was taken of me from a golf trip in February 2006 that I realized just how bad I really looked. I stood with friends of mine and while I didn't look obese, I wasn't happy with how I looked.

It took the shock of a photo to get me back into the gym, change my diet, and work really hard towards the original goals I had set. I worked with the original *plan* put in place with my trainer, and followed through on pushing my workouts and eating a proper diet. By July 2006 I had reached my goal while losing nearly 70 pounds in the process!

One of the greatest gifts we have as humans is the ability to take ourselves somewhere else during times of high stress, boredom, or reflection. Our ability to dream is a gift which allows us the opportunity to visualize how things could be under the optimum circumstances. One of my dreams was to be a smaller version of myself. Another dream I have is to see my children grow and raise families of their own. Some of my dreams have come true and others haven't, but that doesn't stop me from dreaming about opportunities in the future. As you enter retirement, your dreams will play a vital role in the shaping of your retirement. Whether all of your dreams come true will depend upon several factors but two that must be present are planning and the *goals* you set for you and your family.

At some point in your working life, you've dreamed about the life you envisioned for yourself and your family at retirement. Many of these dreams are definitive. When I retire, I'm buying a vacation home. When I retire, I will spend more time with my grandchildren. Dreams are easy to envision but can only get you so far in life. The difficulty comes in making dreams a reality.

For example, many of us dream of winning a lottery and what we would do with millions of dollar, but in order for this dream to become a reality, we must establish a plan of action and have goals that can tell us whether our plan is getting us closer to our dreams. So the common action is to buy a lottery quick pick ticket and see if we win. Once we realize that we didn't win by doing a quick pick, we may decide to change our tactics by picking specific numbers. We continue a variety of methods until it's discovered that we've wasted valuable dollars on this dream.

Successful individuals will tell you they reached where they are today by envisioning their future, establishing a plan of action, and setting goals to monitor their progression. The dreams you have can only get you so far in life. If you are serious about securing your retirement and seeing your retirement dreams become a reality, it's imperative you take the time to *plan* a course of action that will bring you closer to your dreams. The planning process serves as a blueprint towards mapping routes which ultimately bring you closer to your dreams. It's certainly possible that you could reach your dreams without planning, but are you willing to risk your retirement?

Don't worry about what others may have. You never know what may be achieved. In some cases you may reach your dreams quickly, in other cases, you may never reach them at all, but unless you have a plan in place, you may never have a chance to reach your retirement dreams.

Once you have a plan in place you need feedback that your plan is getting you closer to your dreams. Any plan should have *goals* that will monitor your progression toward your dreams. The goals you set should start very small in order to build momentum and confidence. The confidence you gain from reaching goals can build as you set new goals which can help you realize your dreams in a faster fashion. Goals are able to be used in accordance with an action plan and can be monitored daily, weekly, monthly, or on yearly basis. The goals we set for ourselves compliment that action statements and plans which remind us of what needs to be done in order to make the vision in our mind become a reality.

Once you're retired you should never stop dreaming, planning, and setting goals. It's great that you've reached one important summit in your life, but your journey continues. Take the time to reflect on where you would like to see your life in the future. Find some quiet time and share your dreams with your spouse and family. This should be one of the most exciting times of your life and it can be through proper planning and goal setting.

3

Driving Without a Road Map

The year was 1976 and my family and I were on our way to Walt Disney World. For most of my life our vacations were trips to visit the grandparents and cousins, but this trip would be a real vacation that included traveling to a different state, staying at a hotel that had a pool, and eating at restaurants. Needless to say, the prospects of visiting a place like Disney World itself was simply icing on the cake.

You see I grew up in the prototypical middle class family. My parents worked hard for every dollar they earned and didn't believe in borrowing money for a trip you couldn't pay for. They had always dreamed about taking the family to a place such as Disney World, but in order to do this it would require careful planning and the establishment of goals in order to make this dream a reality.

In 1971 my parents began saving for the trip. They had estimated how much money they would need to pay for the trip and determined that they may have enough funds by the spring of 1976. In order to stay on track they set goals along the way. Sometimes these goals were achieved, other times something happened where the money was needed elsewhere and set them back, but they never lost focus on the ultimate prize. Finally after two years of saving, we began planning our journey to the Magic Kingdom.

Planning of our trip began with the basics such as how long we would stay, where we would stay, how we would travel, how long it may take, and what other sites we should visit along the way. As the discussions began all of us were excited about the opportunity to fly to Florida, stay at Disney's Contemporary Resort and visit the park for a week, but it was quickly decided we would drive to Florida, stay at a Day's Inn, and visit the park for four days. In essence, compromises were made in order to reach our original goal.

Our family had never taken a vacation of this sort that required so much planning. My father had to spend time each night before the trip reading through road maps in order to determine the fastest route. He estimated the amount of time we could drive, where we would stay the night and places we may visit along the way. The road map provided him with detailed information that kept him on course towards our ultimate goal.

I share this history with you because in many respects the path to retirement is no different than planning a trip to Disney World. It's possible that you and your family could reach the Magic Kingdom on your own without the assistance of a plan or map, but how long would it take? How much would it cost? How many detours would you have along the way? How long could you afford to stay? What other experiences would you face along the way? Retirement is often called a journey, but are you willing to risk your retirement without a proper map or plan to follow?

The amount of time you spend in retirement could be just as long as the amount of time it took for you to get married, raise your children, and get them through college. Think about all the life experiences you had during that period. Think about how the cost of everything went up exponentially during that period. While you may think that you may only have a few short years together in retirement, you have to plan for contingencies. This is not to say you don't spend money and go in a shell; it simply means you utilize your resources in such a way in order to ensure that your money outlives you, not the other way around.

Not everyone's roadmap is going to work out perfectly. Detours will occur along the way. Just as there are times you may have had a flight delay, a hotel sold out, or you've had car trouble, things will not go according to plan. You may find yourself in a position where interest rates or the markets drop dramatically and you will need to react along the way. What's important is that you review your Personal Retirement Road Map and choose an alternative plan that saves you the most TIME and MONEY.

If you're investments are progressing according to plan, you can make adjustments to catch up. If you're progressing faster than you thought, you can consider adding new dreams or goals or reduce your investment risk exposure.

Whatever the situation your road map will provide you with an up to date accounting as to where you are.

How Do I Create a Personal Retirement Road Map?

Just as my parents dreamed of taking our family to Walt Disney World, they realized that it would require much more than hope to get our family there. In the initial stages, my parents never presented the idea of taking a trip to Disney. I believe they knew that if they broached the subject, and it turned out it wasn't possible, we would be devastated.

My parents began with a broad vision. They considered the time of year we would want to go, the amount of time we would stay there, and ways they could save money so we could spend more time or visit other sites along the way. These considerations were written on paper and then prioritized based upon what would be more exciting for us. In essence they created an outline of the trip.

Once they had an outline, the real work began as they considered the cost associated with the trip. They received a great deal of information from Disney, hotels in the area, and looked at maps to the Sunshine state. They included ticket fees, transportation costs, eating and lodging allowances, and miscellaneous expenses. Once these costs were estimated, they were able to calculate a daily budget for the trip and the saving process began.

If you're a pre-retiree, then you're looking for answers as to "when" and "if" you will be able to retire in the timeframe you've imagined. If you are retired and you've already begun your journey to the Magic Kingdom, you may need to rely on information that will ensure you that you have enough money to make it home. Whatever your circumstance, it's important you know exactly where you are on your journey through retirement and one of the best ways to do this is to rely on a Road Map that can shed some light.

The best way to begin creating your own Personal Retirement Road Map is to spend some time with a notepad and some quiet time with your spouse. Begin with the big picture. Identify your dreams, the things you would like to do during retirement. According to the Employee Benefit Research Institutes latest research study in 2007, retirees have a great deal of interest in traveling, spending time with family, and participating in hobbies. These may or may not interest you, but discover the things you've put off in life. Take this opportunity to see if they can become a reality.

Once you have a vision of what you would like to do, then you're ready to create an outline and consider practical matters. Here are some key questions you need to consider.

- What is really important to me (money, wealth, happiness, family, kids, travel, etc)?
- What special dreams do I have that I want to achieve before I die?
- What hobbies and interests do I and my spouse want to continue after retirement? What new ones do we want to pick up?
- Am I successful in managing against an annual or monthly cash flow budget?
- How do I balance spending today vs. saving for tomorrow?
- When do I want to retire?

Retirement Planning

- What annual income do I want in retirement? How will inflation impact that number?
- How much of a retirement nest-egg do I need so that my spouse and I can't outlive our income needs, given that one or both of us may live 30 years in retirement?
- Am I currently maximizing my tax deferred savings? (401(k), IRA, etc.)
- Will my employer-provided retirement plan be sufficient?
- What role might Social Security play in my retirement?
- Do I want to continue working after I'm retired?

Investment Planning and Asset Allocation

- Will my current assets grow to a level to meet my wealth needs?
- Is my portfolio appropriately diversified?

- Have I identified an asset allocation and investment management philosophy that will allow me to accumulate wealth within the risk parameters that I'm comfortable with?
- Do I have adequate emergency savings should I lose my job, become disabled, etc?
- How should I think about any executive compensation or stock options that I have?

Estate Planning

- What would happen to my family if I die tomorrow? A year from now?
- Have I adequately protected my family's standard of living if I die?
- Do I have a current will so that my assets and belongings go to the people I choose?
- Have I named guardians for my minor children should I die?
- How do my heirs inherit my money with the least amount of taxation?
- Do I have a current living will, durable power of attorney, and health care proxy?

College Funding

- Do I plan to help my children educate their children?
- What will a year of college cost 5, 10, 15, or 20 years from now?
- What nest-egg do I need to accumulate to meet college costs for grandchildren? What is the best way to accumulate these funds (parent, child, Section 529, etc)

Insurance and Risk Management

- Do I have sufficient health, disability, liability, homeowner, and automobile insurance? Should I consider a liability umbrella policy?
- Do I have adequate life insurance to protect my family?
- How can I protect my assets from a major medical disaster?

- Should I consider long-term care insurance? Do I have a history of strokes/disabilities in my family?

- What would happen if I became disabled?

<u>Income Tax Planning</u>

- Am I paying the least amount of income taxes possible?

- Am I maximizing my possible deductions?

- Do I have a tax-efficient investment portfolio that is minimizing my taxes?

Once you've determined how many of these questions may impact your retirement life, you can proceed with finding a Road Map that can fit your needs. The Road Map you select today may need updating in the future. What is important is that you take the time to find one and begin the planning of your retirement dreams.

Where Can I Get Help Building My Personal Retirement Road Map?

Today many investment firms provide their clients with a snapshot into their future through their financial planning tools. While many of these services are beneficial to the client, in many cases the client doesn't have the access to make adjustments or changes to the plan on his own. These financial planning tools are kept within the firm so that the advisor monitors the progression of their retirees over time and relates the information to the retiree. They provide updated statements which explain portfolio performance and provide a snapshot of their progression towards their goals.

These plans can be very helpful to retirees but I can understand why these firms do not provide access to their clients, and why retirees would like to have access to this information. The investment firm would like to see the retiree invest for the long term, but retirees who are looking to protect their nest egg have a tendency to review their progression almost on a daily basis. They feel they cannot accept losses and it keeps them up at night. I can tell you from experience when this occurs, your finances are ruling your life versus you ruling your finances.

There are certain times you need to review your Personal Retirement Road Map. Many of these will occur during a life event such as the loss of a job, a health concern, or needing to help family members, but most of the time, you really only need to review your Personal Retirement Road Map about twice a year. If you find yourself constantly review your road map after the close of every market's session, the time you spend in front of a computer or spreadsheet will be lost time, which is something you can't afford. It's not healthy and in most cases is unnecessary. We will review in another chapter the times you need to review your Personal Retirement Road Map, but unless there is a life event that could impact you immediately, let your investments do their job.

I believe the best place to find a Personal Retirement Road Map that fits your needs is to consider the services of working with a qualified financial advisor or planner. Many investment firms today and financial planning firms have the capabilities to create a Personal Retirement Road Map for their clients. The services of these firms have improved over the years and many now provide clearer pictures for clients to see exactly where they are in their journey through retirement. Many retirees are so careful not to spend their assets in anticipation of needing them in the future. If they understand that they are progressing towards their dreams and goals according to their plan, then it affords them the opportunity to consider pursuing new dreams they may have never envisioned for themselves.

Most investment firms offer the ability for you to create your own Personal Retirement Road Map, it's up to you to seek these firms out and find someone who you believe is capable of helping you navigate through retirement.

If you are not comfortable working with a financial professional who can build a Personal Retirement Road Map then an excellent resource you should consider is the services provided by Torrid Technologies (www.torrid-tech.com). Torrid Technology offers a fantastic Retirement Savings Planner which provides you with a realistic view of where you are today and the probability of having enough assets to do the things you dream of in retirement.

The Torrid Technology retirement saver and planner provides immediate feedback as to whether the dreams you have for yourself in retirement are achievable by considering several factors. The retirement saver includes income from Social Security, Pensions, and retirement assets. It gathers information concerning your current expenses, future expenses, and other expenses such as insurance premiums and taxes, and calculates how inflation will impact these costs in the future. The retirement saver considers assets you currently own, assets that may come to you in the future, and evaluates how these assets could impact your retirement years. The Torrid Technology retirement saver and planner provides a detailed spreadsheet so you are able to see the growth of your assets over time and evaluate whether you are closer to reaching your dreams or whether adjustments may need to be made. In essence, the Torrid Technology Retirement Saver and Planner serves as your Personal Retirement Road Map to your dreams.

The program also helps identifies where shortfalls may exist and calculates the additional amount of savings or income you will need over your life in order to make your dreams a reality. The cost of this software is very low and has been recommended by more than ninety percent of the retirees who have used the planner. Torrid Technology is providing an opportunity for you to try their planner by visiting their website at www.torrid-tech.com and clicking the area which has this books title. If you are not working with a financial representative who offers a service of this type, you should absolutely consider their offer.

Another resource you could consider in order to build your Personal Retirement Road Map is the resources available through AARP. AARP provides some basic planning tools you can use along with printable spreadsheets you can use if you're needs aren't as demanding and you're not comfortable using computer programs. The AARP website (www.aarp.org) also provides recommendations of other retirement planning tools.

These are just a few ideas as to where you could find and create your own Personal Retirement Road Map. Just as not all maps are the same, neither will Personal Retirement Road Maps. Some maps will be more detailed than others. It truly depends on your needs, goals, investments, income, and lifestyle, but you won't know for sure if you're able to reach them until you begin the process of putting them down on paper.

Putting your dreams down on paper will be vital to your success in retirement. It's possible that your dreams will be reached without issues, but life is full of surprises. As you begin the planning process remember that unexpected events could occur during your journey. If a particular dream isn't reached, consider alternative strategies that could offer reward in other ways. By having contingencies in place and preparing for life's events, you should be able to react quicker in order to get you back on the road towards the dreams you have in mind for you and your family without costing you a great deal of time or money.

4

Practice Retirement First

One of the greatest ambitions for a sixteen year old is to get their drivers license. The ability to drive promotes a sense of independence, especially when they are behind the wheel for the first time. They are responsible for making the car move, choosing the route, and determining how fast they can go. Excitement is in the air, but this new found independence brings a level of fear and in trepidation.

Retirement is no different. You could encounter many questions that will keep you up at night as you consider or enter retirement. You may not recall, but it's likely you had just as many questions when you got behind the wheel and practiced your driving skills with a parent. You asked the question, they provided the answer based upon their experience and knowledge. As you continued to practice, your knowledge expanded and your confidence grew as you prepared to drive on your own.

How many times have you retired? Hopefully you've only retired once, but if you've retired more than once, it may be because you didn't *practice* your retirement before you decided to retire. If this sounds confusing to you, consider this explanation.

Retirees today have more options than retirees of just twenty five years ago. According to census data, at the turn of the century the average life expectancy for Americans was sixty years old. Retirees sixty years ago didn't face the same issues that most retirees face today. At the turn of the century retirees had not heard about Social Security, most didn't own vacation homes, and they didn't have life saving drugs or healthcare that extended their lives. In many cases, they relied on family for support and shelter.

The concerns that affected your parents will unlikely affect you. Retirees of the today will be able to enjoy a much longer retirement than they've ever imagined. While it's true as we get older our bodies aren't as reliable as they once were, advances in medicine and the healthier lifestyles have extended life expectancy. Every decade census data points out that the average lifespan of men and women continues to grow. Recent studies have indicated that a married couple at age sixty five could live well into their nineties. You may not realize it, but once you hit that magic mark of sixty five, you could live another twenty five years which is about the same amount of time it took for you to have kids, put them through school, and watch them get married, all over again.

The age old saying *practice makes perfect* should be heeded before you make major changes in your lifestyle as you enter retirement. It's important that you understand how major changes such as moving to another state, leaving your job early, or taking up an expensive hobby could have on your retirement happiness. As you enter retirement, you should expect a period of adjustment to the way your life used to be. The completion of your Personal Retirement Road Map should help you determine if some of your dreams are attainable, but nothing compares to taking these dreams for a trial run.

Here are some recommendations you could consider before taking to the open road into retirement.

1. Take longer vacations. Fill your days with golf, travel, or leisure activities that you anticipate doing in retirement. If you can come back from your vacation longing for another adventure, this should be an important item you want to include in your retirement road map.

2. Spend more time with friends and family. See how important their relationship will be to you in the future. How will your or your friends moving impact your life. Do you have grandchildren you want to spend more time with? Can you help your kids with their hectic life?

3. Retirees may feel compelled to move closer to family, a warmer climate, or a retirement community. Before you make such a move you may want to consider a renting versus owning. If moving closer to your family, a warmer climate or into a retirement community is part of your retirement dream, then take the time to rent space before you pack up and move.

The last thing you have in mind is to pack your belongings and move to a place where you could be miserable. Some of the more popular retirement destinations such as Florida, Texas, and Arizona can be unbearable during the summer. If you feel that you would like to move to one of these popular spots for the remainder of your retirement, consider renting space during the summer and see if you could really tolerate the heat.

When it comes to relationships with children and grandchildren, everyone is different. Prior to retirement you wished you could spend more time with your family, but now that you have free time on your hands, how much time are you willing to offer? If spending more time with your children and grandchildren are part of your retirement dreams, then before you make the move to get closer to them, you may want to test the waters first and make sure this is really what both of you want. Consider renting in a nearby community where you could be closer to your grandchildren, help if needed, but not serve as a crutch for your children. I've heard it many times. One of the greatest joys of having grandchildren is that you can always give them back to their parents, but if you're too close it could be like children all over again.

Many retirees choose to stay right where they are. They are surrounded by friends and a community they enjoy. If you're happy with where you are living today, don't feel compelled that you need to move. There will be plenty of opportunities for you to rent homes and apartments that are furnished for a finite amount of time. By choosing to rent, you could not only satisfy some of your dreams, but make sure you have a place to call home.

If you're thinking about moving to a new location, investigate the area by subscribing to their local paper or searching the internet for information about the community such as crime rates, climate, community services, and activities for retirees. Take trips to these areas and spend time talking with residents who have retired. Consult with other retirees as to the reasons they chose this development and what they would have done differently. By listening to those who have gone before you could save you from making mistakes that could have been avoided.

4. Sign up for a subscription to a retirement magazines and internet sites such as AARP. These informational outlets provide great articles about how other retirees are saving, spending their time, destination choices, etc. AARP offers out-

standing insight and advice to those individuals who are about to embark in unchartered territory. The magazine and website provide information that can help you make decisions that are in your families best interest and avoid many pitfalls that may face you.

5. Prior to your retirement, live off a budget and monitor your expenses for as long as possible. It's important that you have an idea as to the amount of outflow you have today in order to understand the amount of inflow you will need to sustain the lifestyle to which you've become accustomed. Invest in a software program where you can track your expenses and code checks that are written. This helps by not only allowing you to see where you may be wasting money, but it provides you with a snapshot of what your income will need to be during retirement.

The spending habits you have prior to retirement will not change very much, so if you have an idea of where the money is going you transition into retirement could be just another day in your life.

6. If you have an interest in working after you're retired, take up a part time job on the weekends to determine if you would really enjoy working at the Home Depot or Wal-Mart. If you wanted to do charity work, devote some time to a local charity and see if there may be an opportunity in the future for future employment.

7. Become serious about pursuing your special interests. If you've always wanted to play golf, learn to play the piano, go back to school take the time to begin the process.

8. Serve as a resource to community organizations such as the YMCA, Chamber of Commerce, High Schools and Universities or business owners. Consult with these groups to see if they may have an interest in utilizing your skills to help others or help their business grow. Ask them about hiring you for a position on a part time basis. The limited time you provide to these organizations could make all the difference in their success, and provide you with an outlet to stay intellectually active.

9. Inquire about grants or fellowships from the government or non profit organizations that allow you to do volunteer work in another part of the country or world for a period of time.

Whether you take the time to follow these steps or have other ideas, the point is to test drive retirement while you still have resources to fall back on. Would you consider buying a new car without test driving it first? Take this opportunity to take up certain hobbies and interests, and investigate whether the changes you've dreamed about are in the best interest of you and your family. What you may find is that by practicing or taking retirement on a test drive, you could save yourself and your family precious time and money you will want in retirement.

5

How Much Income Will I Need in Retirement?

Pat and Lynn Garrett are living in exciting times. After working forty years for the local car dealership, Pat finally decided it was time for a change. He announced his retirement and began pursuing his retirement dreams.

Pat and Lynn have been married for more than forty years. They met in high school and became college sweethearts. Lynn taught school for more than thirty years and when their last child completed college, she announced her retirement and began teaching piano in her home.

The Garrett's raised three children who have all grown and spread about the country. They have four grandchildren and look forward to seeing them anytime they can. They enjoy music and NASCAR. Anytime they can get away to see a race they will go. Pat has always had the desire to purchase a motor coach and travel to NASCAR tracks to watch races over the weekend, but his job kept him from getting away. That's all changed now that Pat has decided to retire, but does he have enough income that will allow him to pursue this dreams?

Pat's situation is similar to many retirees today. His wife is receiving a pension from the school system, but he was never offered a pension. Prior to his retirement, Pat's income covered most expenses such as mortgage payments, college expenses, and everyday living expenses. Lynn was able to save her pension over the past ten years and they have built a nice nest egg, but they not only question if they could afford a motor coach, but it they will have enough money to outlive them in retirement.

One of the most difficult tasks that Pat and Lynn will have as retirees is to determine if the amount of income they have coming from pensions, Social Security, or investments will be enough to maintain their standard of living. Many retirees gather information from magazines, books, and the internet in order to gauge how much income they may need during retirement. Many rely on formulas or the experience of others to help them decipher what they will need in order to meet their living needs. Unfortunately there is no uniform formula you can rely on. What is necessary is that you create a budget and complete your Personal Retirement Road Map so you have a thorough understanding of your future income needs where this income will be coming from.

If you were to pole a group of retirees representing three age groups (55–65), (66–78), and (79–90), and ask them what percentage of their pre-retirement income are spending today, it's very likely the percentages would be different for every age group. The reason, each one of these age groups has different needs, goals, and wants as they move through retirement.

Retirees who set aside assets in retirement plans or have built up additional assets prior to retirement such as Pat and Lynn can rely on these assets to supplement their retirement income or make major purchases early in their retirement years such as a motor coach or a retirement vacation spot. Unfortunately many retirees have trouble gauging the amount they can use from their assets so that their supplemental income doesn't endanger their standard of living. The tendency is for retirees to draw down only on the dividends and interest paid on their investments, keeping the principle balance in tact. They would rather sacrifice retirement dreams than to watch their principle balance invaded.

Unless you're a multimillionaire where money likely is not concern, the idea of only spending dividends or interest needs to be a distant memory if you have a chance of making it through retirement. If the income you receive from Social Security and pensions isn't enough to maintain your standard of living, you will need to rely upon the total return from your assets in order to reach your dreams in retirement.

Years ago, the average retirement period for a retiree was approximately fifteen years. Today the amount of time that a retiree could spend in retirement could be twice that amount. Managing your investments over that period of time could be a daunting task, but if you follow recommendations provided in other chapters of this book, you could have an opportunity to truly enjoy the golden years of retirement.

A second reason that retirees may have a difficult time determining how much income they will need in the future is the affect of taxes and inflation. If you are married and are under the age of sixty five, according to the updated longevity calculations (Society of Actuaries Annuity 2000 Mortality Tables), a sixty five year old man today has a 53 percent chance of living to age eighty five and a 34 percent change of reaching age ninety. A sixty five year old female has a sixty five percent change of living to age eighty five and a 25 percent chance of living to age ninety four. As a couple where both the man and the woman are age sixty five or less, there is a 63 percent probability that one of you will make it to age ninety, and a 36 percent chance that someone will live until age ninety five. I state this simply because if you are married and are retired or nearing retirement, the possibility of one of you living until age ninety is very high. If you consider how much medical care is costing Americans today, what do you believe it will be like twenty five years from now?

Think back twenty years and the cost of a hospital stay, a visit to the doctor, or prescription drugs. Barring a dramatic change in our health care system and policies, it's likely these trends will continue and the price of medical care will continue to rise. While Medicaid may help, the potential tax burden may be just as devastating.

Inflation and taxes serve as a cancer on your money eating away at your buying power. They affect everything in our economy and you need to account for them within your Personal Retirement Road Map. It's important to have your investments working in areas of the marketplace that can outpace inflation to help you maintain your standard of living. If not, you may find yourself in a position where you are dipping into principle balances sooner than you wanted.

Retirement Stages

Another consideration to help you determine the amount of income you may need in the future is to understand the stages of retirement you will enter. Just as you've gone through different stages in your life from a young married couple to a family to now having an empty nest, there are stages to retirement that you should understand.

There are three distinct stages in a retired persons' life. Each of them will require different income requirements and will likely cause a retiree to re-evaluate their investment objectives, goals, and needs. As you go through these stages, it's important to rely on your personal retirement road map as you enter a new stage and update your anticipated needs and goals for the coming years. Things that were important to you when you first retired such as fixing up the house, taking trips to foreign countries or taking up a new hobby may not be as important to you at age seventy five. At age seventy five healthcare costs, long term care, or considering an assisted living home may be more important. Here are some of the various stages you will encounter along the way.

Stage 1: Early Retirement (Age 55–64)

This is the stage of your life where you need to make a decision as to whether you continue working the same job or consider the other options available to you in fields where you have more interest. During this stage, you are likely to remain with your current employer until you can reach Medicare benefits. Health coverage for you and your family will be very important and this could keep you working longer than you wanted.

During this period you are maximizing your savings to the fullest. Usually at this point many of your children are grown and college has been completed. You are at a stage where you realize you must do something and you begin to save more of your income for the years ahead. You may consider projects to update your house or consider looking at a vacation home or recreational vehicle to occupy your time in the future.

If you've decided to retire at this age, you are likely spending more time traveling and doing the things you've delayed until now. You have many ideas you want to explore and this is likely to cause a drain on your cash and investments until you're able to realize pension benefits or Social Security income.

In the near future you are likely to have additional cash flow available other than Social Security or pensions as you consider selling your home and downsizing, selling a business, or receiving an inheritance. The new capital that you receive will provide a boost to your retirement assets and may generate additional income or investment gains to be drawn at a later date.

You don't have many concerns at this point in your life as you tend to be happy with your health and become more health conscious.

As you enter this stage educate yourself on the mistakes others may have made. Talk with co-workers, friends, or family members, and find out some of the issues and concerns they had as they entered this stage of retirement and ask them what they would have done differently. Inquire about the opportunities they missed. This type of information could be invaluable to you as you try to avoid as many mistakes as possible in your decisions.

Stage 2: Retired (Age 65–77)

At this point you're well into retirement and now you're able to share your knowledge with other friends and relatives who may be entering the retirement phase soon. As you progress through these years, you may find that the income needs you had just a few years ago aren't as demanding. You've become comfortable with the amount of income you have and you are enjoying your time in retirement more than ever. Your travel costs may decline a bit here as you choose to stay home and closer to grandchildren.

While income needs may not be fresh on your mind, you may begin to prepare yourself for potential health issues that may become more prevalent. This is also the time you may be considering estate planning and living wills to help reduce the burden on your children and reduce potential estate taxes.

Stage 3: Senior (Age 78–90+)

The asset allocation of your portfolio may dramatically change during this stage as the income needs and preservation of capital become more important. During this period you should make sure that all your estate planning documents are in accordance with current tax laws and a living will is up to date. You may also choose to consider an active gifting strategy in order to reduce the size of your taxable estate so that more of your assets transfer to those you love.

Any gifting plan should be done in accordance with your Personal Retirement Road Map. If the goals you have set for this stage of your life correspond with your road map, then by all means use this opportunity to begin transferring assets to those you love or those charitable entities who have meant so much to you over the years, but don't start the process until your road map verifies that you can afford to give away your assets.

One caveat you should be aware of are the Medicare and Medicaid rules. According to current law many gifts will be disallowed if they were made in an attempt to avoid paying for long term care or health costs. There are some families who try to remove the ownership of assets away from their parents in order to have Medicaid cover long term care costs versus the immediate family. The federal government has become more involved in following the transfer of assets amongst family members over the years and has gone back to the families to collect funds that should have been used to cover long term care costs. The current law will disallow many gifts that were made as late as five years ago to your children or other entities and may hold them accountable for medical expenses that may not have been paid. There are some assets which are excluded by this law. Later chapters discuss current tax laws and actions you could consider to ensure that a majority of your assets transfer to your family legally instead of the government.

How to Determine Income Needs Before Retirement

Pat and Lynn are one of the more fortunate retirement couples. Over the past forty years, they have been able to set aside savings for retirement, but many retirees still find themselves living paycheck to paycheck. These retirees never took the time to budget their expenses over the years and thus find themselves in new territory estimating what their expenses may be in the years ahead. **Don't make this mistake.**

While you're still working, if your household isn't living on a budget that you can see the monthly inflows and outflows, then start one now. It's important you understand where money is being spent. This action will not only provide you with an estimation of your future expenses such as utilities, taxes, and food, but it may also open your eyes to the wasteful nature many Americans have when it comes to spending money.

One of the easiest ways to begin the process is to invest in a software program that will help you budget your household automatically. Many banks and brokerage firms allow direct deposit and bill paying services for their customers. These services allow you to pay your bills online and provide you with a daily account on where your money is going. These accounts are very easy to set up and will serve as an invaluable historical reference for you to determine your expected outflows versus your inflows.

If you're not comfortable with the services provided by the financial institutions, then start keeping a record today of your income and expenses on a spreadsheet, ledger, or whatever means you are comfortable with so you can actually see what your income and expenses are prior to retirement.

If you have an idea of what your income will be after retirement (drawing from pension, investments, Social Security, etc.), then its fine to focus on your current expenses. This information will help you determine if you have enough income to continue a standard of living that is comfortable for you and your family.

In your first few years of retirement don't be shocked if you blow out your expense budget. Pat and Lynn want to purchase a motor coach to travel the NASCAR circuit. These coaches can cost several hundred thousand dollars. While they may have saved enough to cover the purchase of the coach, did they consider expenses associated with the coach such as fuel, maintenance, and insurance? Expenses can be higher during the first stage of retirement as you take advantage of your freedom to do some of the things you've always wanted to do. You may find yourself dipping into more of your investment nest egg than what you had originally planned. If you're Personal Retirement Road Map anticipated this, don't let this cause you stress. At some point in the future, your income and expense needs will level out in order to provide a more predictable retiree pattern.

Once you have a grasp of your potential income and outflows during retirement, review your Personal Retirement Road Map and find deficiencies. Having a dream is great, but remember planning and goal setting. If you do not have sufficient assets to reach your dream, you will need to modify your plan or your dream. I encourage you to visit www.torrid-tech.com. This valuable retirement planner not only forecasts how your retirement assets can grow in the future, but allows you to forecast just how much income you will need in the future to account for taxes and inflationary pressures.

What if I'm already retired?

If you've already retired and in you're in one of the stages listed above, remember it's never too late to right the ship. If there is a leak somewhere in the ship, you can keep sailing along, but eventually water will overtake the boat and you're sunk so it's important to find the expenses that are sinking you!

In many cases these leaks come from not following a household budget. If you do not have a household budget, create one immediately. Just as retirement dreams are hard to reach without proper planning, you can't correct an error unless you understand where the error is coming from.

Follow the budget over the next several months. If you're comfortable, establish an online account with a bank or investment firm which allows you to have all your income come into the account as well as check writing and credit card expenses. Review your statements on a monthly basis in order to determine where your leak may be and take the proper steps to fix the leak.

In some cases it may be unanticipated expenses, in other cases it may be underperforming investments or an asset allocation mix that is not keeping up with inflationary pressures. Whatever the reason, it's important that you find the reason and fix it. The sooner you fix the issue the sooner you can get back to enjoying your retirement and knowing you will have enough money to outlive you.

6

Finding More Income

If a poll were conducted and individuals were asked to name their favorite type of day, it's likely birthdays, anniversaries, and Saturday's would be at the top of the list, but a day that most retirees would likely put at the top of the list would be any day they received a check in the mail!

While many are looking forward to telling their boss to take this job and shove it, it may be in your best interest to consider some other options that could provide additional income to your household and ensure that your golden years are golden. These options could not only provide additional income during retirement, but could provide additional benefits.

Here are suggestions which may allow you to retire when you want and provide additional income to the household during retirement.

1. Find a Hobby that Pays!

You've just retired and the last thing you want to think about is going back to work again to cover household expenses, but maybe you could consider a new hobby that not only interests you as well, but pays the bills as well.

You've been dreaming about retirement for years, but the anxiety of not knowing if you'll have enough to survive is not worth the stress at home. I'm not recommending you continue to stay with the job you've been doing over the past thirty years, but consider working with a company where you can utilize your interests and hobbies and get paid for your work.

Many companies today such as The Home Depot, Walgreen's, Borders, Staples, and many other companies that cater to seniors, may be a great place for you to apply your talent. Some of these companies offer residual benefits such as the opportunity for flexible hours and healthcare coverage. Retirees have attributes that employers want from their co-workers such as reliability, maturity, experience, and a genuine interest to help the customer. A few hours each week could mean a substantial increase in your household income.

Visit the National Employer Team at www.aarp.org/money/careers for employers who are looking for veterans over age fifty.

2.Sell Your Home

Many retirees continue to live in the same neighborhoods where they raised their families. Families who raised their children for the past twenty years have moved on as newer families with younger children move into these neighborhoods to take advantage of the school district, larger space, or other conveniences. While you may have a special place in your heart for your home remember that once you've passed, it's likely your children will put the house on the market in order to disburse your estate. Why not take advantage of the appreciation in your home over the years and trade down to a smaller primary residence. This action could not only lower your maintenance costs, but it could offer additional cash from the sale which could be invested for additional income.

According to Brookings, the average house in the United States has appreciated nearly 7 percent annually since 1945. Over the past several years, due in large part to the stagnancy of the stock market from 2000–2005, home prices and real estate have nearly doubled the average return per year. Eventually, we are likely to see home prices begin to appreciate closer to the norm, but the value of your current home may allow you to trade down to another home that could significantly lower your monthly maintenance costs and provide a surplus of tax free cash to invest for the future.

While selling your house could provide additional income, a residual benefit could be lower expenses to your annual household budget. If you're living in a larger home, the home price may have appreciated to a level where the property taxes become a strain on the household budget. Energy costs may also be a burden, especially if the house is in need for an updated heat and air system or new windows. If you consider downsizing, you may have the opportunity to move into a smaller home that is more efficient, has lower operating expenses, and lower real estate taxes, thus providing you with additional income each month that you can use on you rather than pay to the government or an energy company.

Another benefit to consider downsizing is the current exemption allowed under IRS codes. Currently homeowners are able to use a $500,000 exemption on capital gains on the sale of the home provided it's been owned for two out of five years by the current owner ($750,000 in some states). If you no longer have a mortgage on your home, you could move into a smaller home and invest the difference into investments that provide additional growth or income.

The idea of selling your home where you've spent a great deal of your life raising your children and watching them grow will likely be a very emotional decision. The memories and the hassle of moving are likely large obstacles you and your spouse will need to discuss, but these decisions may not be as severe as the stress created when you run out of money during retirement and you find yourself in a position where you must sell your house or take out a home equity loan in order to make ends meet.

Retirees should understand that long term financial security may be of more value than living with the memories that you can take with you. Life can be much more enjoyable with the reduced burdens of maintenance costs, lower taxes, and the upkeep on a small town home or condominium. Instead of paying to have the lawn cut or trimming bushes, retirees can use those funds to build a financial legacy that could put their grandchildren through school.

3. Consider Condo or Apartments

These days there are several communities that cater to retirees where you can purchase a condo or apartment. By selling your current home and moving into a smaller community, you can reduce the upkeep to your current home along with seeing our utility expenses and perhaps real estate taxes go down. In many circumstances these communities offer luxurious accommodations along with the ability to have your grounds, security, and maintenance and repairs all covered by a monthly fee. Many of these communities are also located close to many shopping venues or hospitals where you may walk to the store or use public transportation. This may afford you to sell one of your cars if you have two in the garage.

If you have considered downsizing into a condo or townhouse, you could use this opportunity to have a garage sale to get rid of a lot of that junk you've collected over the past thirty years. When you're forced to move into a smaller space, you find out just how stuff was collected over the years that you can sell to someone else. Once you sell your home and purchase your new condo, you can use any remaining assets from the sale and allocate these assets investments to provide additional income during retirement.

If you find yourself in a position where you do not have equity from the sale of your home, go ahead and consider moving into a smaller condo anyway. The excess savings from lower utility costs and taxes may be enough to warrant the move.

4. Relocate to nearby community or moving to an affordable part of the country.

In many cases, retirees have already decided where they would like to spend the most time in their retirement years. For some, it's close to family, for others, it's a nice beach or a place close to old friends. If you're fortunate to make that decision and have a place to call home during retirement, great, but other retirees may need to consider moving to another part of the country that is more affordable.

If you happen to live in a part of the country where the cost of living is high consider finding another location or part of the country that offers the opportunity for you to live more affordably and in an area of your choosing. Over the years the pattern has been for many New Yorkers to find a nest in Florida where the weather is warmer and there is no income tax, but Florida has become so popular with their attraction of these snowbirds that costs have raised dramatically over the years. Today many New Yorkers are becoming *half backs* where they move to Florida for a while, but realize it's too expensive for them so they move halfway back to New York to states such as North Carolina or Tennessee, thus the term *half back*.

These states offer many amenities which are appealing to retirees such as lower housing costs, acceptable climates, and affordable tax situations. Before you decide to make a move to a where you've always dreamed about retiring do your research. You can find a lot of information about a community on the web or through various books. You want to carefully consider weather, taxes, healthcare facilities, crime rates, activities, community services, and public transportation.

After you've completed your research take the time to visit the community. You may want to visit retirement communities and speak with the appropriate representatives about their property. Question some of the residents who may live in a specific community and find out why they have made this location their home. Make sure they tell you their likes and dislikes about specific items that would affect you such as traffic, taxes, shopping, and local government initiatives.

Your diligence could be immensely valuable as you determine if the move is in the best interest of you, your spouse, and your family. While it may be important to consider a lower cost community, it is just as vital that you could be comfortable in your new surroundings.

5. Reverse Mortgages

If you're intent on making things work where you live, a Reverse Mortgage may be an option that you can use.

If you own a home and are at least 62, you could get money to pay for unforeseen expenses, buy a new car, cover long-term care needs, or add additional income to the household by taking out a reverse mortgage. Reverse mortgages are loans designed specifically for older homeowners which transforms the equity in a home into liquid cash without having to either move or make regular loan repayments. Reverse mortgages permit house-rich but cash-poor elders a way to use their housing equity to cover household expenses during retirement, pay for home care while they remain in the home or for nursing home care later on, or other cover unforeseen expenses during retirements. Here's how a reverse mortgage works:

In a reverse mortgage, the homeowner applies for a reverse mortgage from a lender (usually a bank). The process is very similar to that of a normal mortgage closing where closing costs will be. Once closing documents are finalized, the homeowner receives a sum of money from the lender based largely on the value of the house, the age of the borrower, and current interest rates. For example, a seventy year old with a $200,000 house in Westchester County, New York, would be able to receive a maximum loan of $103,483 (based on 2005 figures).

The amount you receive will be dependent upon the interest rate and the age of the borrower, so if rates are low, and the borrower is older (over age 70), the amount you could receive may be enough to ensure your standard of living.

The borrowers usually get the money in one of three ways (or in any combination of the three): in a lump sum, as a line of credit that can be drawn on at the borrower's option, or in a series of regular payments, called a *reverse annuity mortgage*. The most popular choice is the line of credit because it allows a borrower to decide when he or she needs the money and how much. Moreover, no interest is charged on the untapped balance of the loan.

Although it is often assumed that an elderly person would want to use the funds from a reverse mortgage loan for health care, there are no restrictions—the funds can be used in any way. For instance, the reverse mortgage could be used to pay back taxes, for house repairs, or to retrofit a home to make it handicapped-accessible.

Borrowers who take out a reverse mortgage still own their home. The loan is usually repaid back to the lender when the last surviving borrower dies, sells the home, or moves out. In addition, the repayment amount cannot exceed the value of the borrower's home at the time the load is repaid.

A reverse mortgage cannot be taken out if there is prior debt against the home. Thus, either the old mortgage must be paid off before taking out a reverse mortgage or some of the proceeds from the reverse mortgage used to retire the old debt.

Reverse mortgages are somewhat underutilized at this time. Only an estimated $60,000—$75,000 of these loans have been made, but financial institutions, sensing an opportunity as the population ages and people live longer lives, are expanding their reverse mortgage programs.

The most widely available reverse mortgage product, and the source of the largest cash advances, is the Home Equity Conversion Mortgage (HECM), the only reverse mortgage program insured by the Federal Housing Administration (FHA). However, the FHA sets a ceiling on the amount that can be borrowed against a single-family house, which is determined on a county-by-county basis. In Westchester County, New York, for example, that ceiling is $260,018 (in

2005). High-end borrowers must look to the proprietary reverse mortgage market, which imposes no loan limits.

Is a Reverse Mortgage Right for You?

While reverse mortgages look like no-lose propositions on the surface, they also have some significant downsides. First, the closing costs for these loans are about double those for conventional mortgages. Closing costs on a reverse mortgage for the $200,000 home described above would be more than $10,000. These costs can be financed by the loan itself, but that reduces the money available to you.

Reverse mortgage payments could affect your eligibility for government benefits, including Medicaid. Generally, these payments will not be counted as income as long as they are spent within the same month that they are received. The funds you receive from a reverse mortgage are not taxable and will not affect your income since it is considered a loan. Likewise, the funds you receive from the reverse mortgage will not affect your eligibility or taxation of Social Security benefits or Medicare benefits, but if the funds are not spent, however, they could accumulate and push your resources over the allowable limits for Medicaid or Social Security eligibility. In addition, payments from *reverse annuity mortgages* may be counted as income for purposes of Medicaid and Social Security income *whether or not* they are spent within the month they are received. This shouldn't be treated as income, since it simply involves withdrawing equity from one's home, but the state may view it differently since the funds come in a regular monthly check. In any case, you should consult with an elder lawyer in your state if you have any concern about how a reverse mortgage will affect your eligibility for federal benefits.

Also, bear in mind that if your major objective is to safeguard an inheritance for your children, a reverse mortgage may not be a good idea. As soon as the elderly person (or the survivor of an elderly couple) dies, it will be necessary to sell the home and much, if not all of the sales proceeds must be paid to the lender, not to mention potential capital gain taxes.

Many lenders will have requirements such as paying your real estate taxes; maintain the repair on your home, and keeping the home insured. These are fairly standard conditions of default on any mortgage, but on reverse mortgages, lenders have the option to pay for these expenses by reducing your loan advances and using the difference to pay these obligations. But if you have a pressing need for additional income and have no close heirs, or if you do not intend to benefit your children or your children don't particularly want to inherit the house, a reverse mortgage can be a way to supplement income, perhaps without jeopardizing Medicaid eligibility.

Reverse mortgages are complex products and borrowers are advised to acquaint themselves with the different options available and then carefully compare competing loan offerings. For more information on reverse mortgages, here are two outstanding Web sites to get you started in that process:

- You can learn the basics about reverse mortgages from the AARP's excellent reverse mortgage Web site. The site includes a calculator for estimating the loan for which a borrower would be eligible. Go to: www.aarp.org/revmort or contact them at 1-800-209-8085.
- For more details, background information, and supplementary materials, visit the National Center for Home Equity Conversion's site at www.reverse.org.

These are just a few solutions that could work for you. The important fact to consider is to plan accordingly. Take the time to review your personal circumstances and discuss your situation with your family. Many times you may find that your family wants you to be happy regardless of where you may have to move, if you may have to go back to work, or if no inheritance is left for them.

6. Take More Investment Risk

Think about this statement. *As retirees inch closer to retirement, their philosophy towards risk becomes more conservative.* Do you think this statement is true?

It's likely you, along with other readers answered this believe this statement is true.

While the thought of consistent income from your retirement assets sounds appealing, the question that many retirees need to ask is, *will I outlive my assets, or will my assets outlive me?* In some cases, the actions you've taken years earlier may leave you in a position where you do not need to go to work, sell your home, or transact a reveres mortgage. A simple reallocation of your investment assets towards more risk may be all that you need in order to ensure a comfortable retirement life for you and your loved ones.

Many retirees believe that once you've retired, they should consider becoming more conservative as it relates to their investments. It's a common practice to assume that as you get closer to retirement, it's time for you to consider reducing the investment risk exposed to your nest egg, and consider using income from the nest. But do you realize that you could be taking on additional risk by allocating your assets to investments which you deem safer?

For more than 30 years you've relied upon the equity and real estate markets to provide you with growth to build your nest egg. Why should things change simply because you're retired? What has suddenly changed within the financial markets to suggest that they will not continue to be profitable?

There will always be volatility within the markets. There will always be *events* which cause huge swings within the market, but the overall trend of the markets over the past two hundred years has been to see our free economy continue to grow returns of 10 percent annually. If you think that you may be living in the next ten year time period where the markets fall every year, then I can understand your concern, but there are other risks that can prove just as detrimental to any nest.

Most investors are aware of risks associated within the stock market, but other risks damaging to their nest over time include inflation, interest rates, and political risks. These risks will influence the performance of any investment portfolio. It doesn't matter if you're invested fully in the stock markets or c.d.'s. These risks will effect your retirement. What's important is that you understand the potential risks and utilize your Personal Retirement Road Map to help you take advantage of opportunities as they present themselves.

What investors fail to realize is that over the long term (ten years or more), the stock market has represented the best historical investment value for investors. Have there been periods when this hasn't been true? Sure, especially if you consider 2000–2002, but if you had followed your Personal Retirement Road Map and made adjustments during key periods such as May and November, you could have avoided many negative events that have taken place over time.

I'm about to give you some insight you're not likely to hear from many individuals who are affiliated with the financial markets. You see, the job of the brokerage community, research analysts, financial websites, magazines, newspapers, and television is to *sell* you information that will lead you to pay for their service, whether directly or through advertising. Don't get me wrong, I'm in this field myself. Some advice is worth it, but for the most part, a lot of what you see, hear, and read today is generated in order to get you to react. These services don't really care which way you react. They profit when the markets go up or down.

I've always had an issue with the media. Do not allow the information you receive from media sources to influence your Personal Retirement Road Map. It's especially dangerous when you have a show that could influence individuals to make financial decisions that could dramatically affect their lives such as CNBC. I believe CNBC should be viewed as a form of television entertainment. While it's true that CNBC provides financial content, they are in the business to generate revenue through the selling of advertising on their network. You should not rely on CNBC to provide you with financial advice that is in YOUR best interest. It doesn't matter whether the markets are fifty points away from a new all time high for the Dow or a new one year low for the Dow Jones Industrial Average. The media whether print or television will hype it in such a way in order to make you feel good or bad about your investments. The last thing they expect is complacency, because when you're complacent, it could mean lower ratings and lower ratings means you're not tuning in, and if you're not tuning in, they can't raise advertising fees.

To illustrate my point, in twenty years within the financial services industry working with major brokerage firms I've taken up the habit of collecting magazine, newspaper headlines, and other books that speak of euphoric or doomsday. Usually when several media outlets jump on board clamoring for readers or viewers, here is what I have experienced; it's either a TOP or BOTTOM for whatever is the conversation of the day.

February 20, 2006, Fortune Magazine front page cover was the demise and potential bankruptcy of General Motors. At the time, the stock was selling for $20 per share; its likely many people read that article and thought about selling all the shares or bonds they owned. I know I had clients who considered this. Six months later, General Motors stock had increased more than fifty percent.

I can share hundreds of other stories just like what happened with General Motors. The point I would like to emphasize is not to allow your emotions to rule your investment decisions or your instincts. Sometimes the best investment decisions you make is when you do nothing at all. In the case of GM shareholders who opted NOT to sell their shares after reading the Fortune article, they were rewarded for their lack of action six months later.

I realize taking on more investment risk may not be appealing to you, but there are chapters (*Chapter 9 Get in Touch with Your Emotions and Chapter 13 Beating the Markets*) which can explain why it will be in your best interest to take on more risk when the opportunities present themselves.

A Case Study on Finding More Income: John and Brenda Summitt

John (60) recently retired from XYZ Corporation after 30 years of service. Brenda has been busy raising 3 children for the past 22 years, but now that the last college tuition check has been sent, they are ready to plan for their retirement.

John's annual income when he retired was $75,000. The Summitt's feel they could comfortably live on a $55,000 annual income during retirement. Things would be a little tight, but they would still have the opportunity to take vacations, fix up their home, and help their children should they need it. John is expected to receive a pension of $23,000 a year from his company. He has $250,000 saved in his 401(k) account and will need to take distributions from the account until he accepts Social Security at age 67.

John and Brenda have a nice four bedroom home in an area of town that is known to be one of the better school districts. They've lived in the same home for the past 20 years and have paid off their mortgage. Recently many homes have been selling in the neighborhood to other families for more than 10 times what John and Brenda originally paid for their home. The average selling price for a home the size of John and Brenda's is about $350,000.

John and Brenda met with their financial advisor to discuss how much John needed to withdraw from his 401(k) each year in order to cover household expenses. According to the advisors' computations, John would need to draw-down over $30,000/year for the next 7 years from his 401(k) in order to meet budget expectations.

After meeting with the advisor, they soon realized that the retirement savings John had accumulated through 20+ years in his 401(k) could be gone within the next 7 years. John and Brenda had serious concerns about whether they should take on another job in order to cover them until John begins collecting Social Security, but neither one of them has any interest in getting back to the workforce.

Solution:

John's advisor suggested selling their primary house and trading down to a smaller brick town home closer to downtown which was listed for $200,000. One of the immediate benefits would be less time and money devoted to maintenance, lower utility and insurance costs, and a 50% reduction in property taxes. The area where John and Brenda had lived for over 20 years was one of the more popular areas in town simply because of the school zone. More and more families were moving in and prices were moving up.

John and Brenda spent $10,000 on fixing up their house and had it listed with a local realtor. Within 2 days, they had 3 contracts on the home. The highest bidding contract was $360,000.

John and Brenda met with their advisor once again to determine whether they should sell their house. The advisor provided the following illustration:

If they paid cash for the town home ($200,000), they could add an additional $133,000 to their investment portfolio, which could be used until John's Social Security began in 7 years, OR they consider a new mortgage on the town home. If they placed 20% down and borrowed against a 10 year interest only loan at 5.5%, the net payment would be $475 per month for the next 10 years.

John and Brenda could invest $293,000 to move into their investment portfolio with $160,000 of the proceeds into a fixed c.d. paying 5.5% for 10 years and receive $733 per month in interest. Once they subtracted the mortgage payment, they still received an additional $3,000 per year in interest for the next 10 years. The remaining $133,000 would be invested in short term c.d.'s paying 5% for the next 7 years in order to meet additional income needs for the household until John turned 67 and began receiving his Social Security benefits.

The advisor also pointed out that due to the smaller home, the average monthly savings from lower real estate taxes, utilities, and maintenance issues on their new home would result in an additional savings of $150 per month. The advisor recommended that John and Brenda both take out long term care policies that provided $150 per day in coverage for both spouses as well as an indexed universal life policy that could pay off the mortgage and increase their estate value for their children.

John and Brenda decided to follow this plan. While the initial move was a hassle and the loss of fond memories was difficult, they moved into a community that offered several other amenities they never had at their older home and met new friends that were similar in to their situation.

After ten years, John and Brenda are living their retirement dream. Their town home has climbed in value by over 50 percent. They used the c.d.'s that were set to mature in 10 years to payoff their mortgage. John's 401(k) account has doubled and now presents them with the opportunity to draw additional income required for minimum distributions. They have long term care insurance to cover them should it be needed along with a universal life policy to help them with estate planning.

By researching all the possibilities available to them prior to John's retirement, the Summitt's aren't living paycheck to paycheck. They have less stress, less work to do around the house, and more time to spend doing what it is they originally dreamed of doing which is living their retirement dream.

7

Getting the Most from Social Security, Medicare, and Medigap

Over the years a concern of new retirees has been whether they will be able to depend upon the payment of Social Security and Medicare benefits. Ever since its creation retirees have always assumed that they could rely upon these benefits during retirement. In recent years the topic of Social Security has served as a lightening rod to encourage senior voters to vote for politicians who support keeping the "trust fund" intact, but the truth of the matter is if you're reading this book and you're over the age of fifty, it's safe to assume that your benefits will be there for you when you need them.

The funds that have been set aside by our government for Social Security recipients are actually held in two separate funds. One fund is used for retirement benefits, disability and survivor benefits. The other is reserved for Medicare. According to the Social Security Administration, if medical costs continue to soar, the Medicare fund will have problems beginning in 2041, but this doesn't mean that benefits would be lost, it simply means that somewhere down the road, Congress is going to need to deal with issues affecting your children and grandchildren, not you.

So since you don't need to worry about losing benefits during your lifetime, here is some helpful information you need to know regarding Social Security and Medicare benefits.

Eligibility Requirements

There are several conditions which must be met in order to be eligible for Social Security benefits. One of these conditions is obviously your age. As of 2007 there are various ages in which you become eligible for full benefits through Social Security. If you were born prior to 1938, the full benefit age is 65. If you were born after 1938, the full benefit age gradually increases to 67, and if you were born after 1959, your full benefit age is 67.

It is possible to receive benefits as early as age 62, but keep in mind, once you begin the process of receiving Social Security benefits, you cannot stop the process. These benefits will be paid at significantly lower level compared to what you could receive by waiting until your full benefit age, but your current financial circumstances may dictate that you take them now.

Another condition which must be met is you must have worked a minimum forty quarters and paid FICA taxes. If you did not work the minimum hours, you may be eligible for benefits through our spouse.

Over the years you may have received information from the Social Security Administration as to the anticipated eligible benefit during your retirement years. This information provides a realistic view as to your expected income benefit during retirement at various distribution ages. Keep in mind that not all benefits are created equal. Your benefit amount is based upon your past income and FICA taxes paid.

Defer or Not to Defer: That is the Question

Not everyone has the flexibility to defer collecting Social Security benefits. According to the Social Security Administration in 2005 a little over 72 percent of all beneficiaries are collecting a reduced benefit because of early retirement. Many of these retirees have no choice, due to economic reasons (e.g., they are unable to work because of health problems or can't find suitable work). Retirees who are fortunate enough to have a choice in the matter, however, must decide whether it is more economically advantageous to collect Social Security early, to collect at the normal retirement age, or to delay after the normal retirement age.

Many new retirees may prefer to receive a dollar from the government now rather than wait for two in 2010. Given the alarms of insolvency sounded by both friends and foes of the program, the retirees' eagerness is understandable, but there are threats already at hand that are much more real and insidious. Earnings from a part-time job in retirement, an investment portfolio generating income or normal life expectancy factors could determine the amount of funds you actually "net" from Social Security if you decide to receive benefits as soon as you are eligible.

Beginning 2007 if a person under "full retirement age" (i.e., 65 years, 10 months in 2007) and has earned income of more than $12,960 while collecting Social Security, the benefits will be reduced $1 for every $2 earned above the threshold. In the year in which you reach full retirement age, these benefits will be reduced by $1 for every $3 earned over $34,400.

What many retirees fail to realize is that Social Security benefits can be reduced based upon the income, interest, and dividends you receive? If you have *combined income* from other sources that account for $25,000—$34,000 as an individual, then fifty percent of your Social Security benefits could be taxed. If your income is over $34,000, up to 85 percent of your benefits could be taxed. If you're filing as a couple, the limits are $32,000—$44,000 (50%), and $44,000 (85%). Combined income is determined by the following equation: adjusted gross income plus taxable interest plus one half of your Social Security benefits equals combined income. If this number puts you over a limit, you may want to consider strategies to keep more of the benefits you are receiving from Social Security. If you don't mind paying up to 85 percent of the benefits back to the government then by all means do nothing, but if you'd like to get some of the Social Security tax you've paid over the past forty years back, take steps to reduce your income as much as possible. More information concerning the taxation of benefits you may visit www.ssa.gov/planners/taxes.htm or contact the Social Security Administration.

In order to determine when is the best time to take Social Security benefits ask yourself this question first, do I need them now? Would your life be better by having income coming into the household now or could you afford to wait a few years until you reach your normal retirement age, which according to the Social Security Administration is age 65 if you were born before 1937, age 66 if you were born before 1943, and 67 if you were born after 1960. If you find yourself in a position where Social Security income will help you now then don't defer. Anything you can do to relieve financial pressures to the household should come first, but here are some options to consider that may make holding off on benefits a viable option.

According to Dr. Thomas Dalton, Professor of Accounting at the University of San Diego, people who defer collecting Social Security beyond their normal retirement age will receive a full monthly retirement benefit, depending on how long benefits are delayed. People who reach normal retirement age on or after 2008, the increase for each month of delay is two-thirds of one percent of the full retirement benefit, or an 8 percent increase for each year of delay.

For example, if a person would have received $1,000 per month by retiring at his or her normal retirement age of 66, that person would receive $1,160 per month by waiting twenty four months (or age 68) and $1,320 per month by waiting forty eight months (or age 70) to collect Social Security. Delaying benefits past age 70, however, adds nothing to a person's monthly benefit so you need to start drawing benefits at age seventy.

The percentage increase is less, on a sliding scale, for people reaching normal retirement age prior to 2008, dropping to a percent increase for each year of delay for retirees reaching normal retirement age prior to 1982. So the bottom line is this: Unless you are receiving a guaranteed return of 10 percent or more on your investment portfolio or retirement assets for the next four to five years, you are better to wait to accept taking benefits until age 70, because at age 76, the benefits you would have received for the past six years would then overtake the total amount of reduced benefits you would have received if you began taking benefits at age 62.

In my experience, I've seen it all and in all situations, it was based upon different factors. Some retirees had a history of poor health in their families and didn't feel they would see age eighty. Others chose to take an early distribution while their spouse chose to hold off until age seventy. Some retirees chose a part time job to work which would have equated to the benefits they would have received, and delayed their benefits until their normal retirement age. Some never needed the additional income and waited until age seventy.

I have concerns with individuals who choose to receive Social Security benefits at age 62 and take distributions from their retirement account, especially if their household income reaches above $32,000 for joint filers. While I understand as a retiree you want as much income as possible, taking distributions from your retirement assets could cause the benefit you receive from Social Security to be taxed each year until you reach normal retirement age.

It is estimated that as much as 85 percent of your Social Security benefits could be reduced if your income breaches the threshold determined by the Social Security Administration. If you find yourself debating as to whether you should take distributions from your retirement account or delay Social Security benefits, delay your benefits. The only exception to this rule would be if your retirement account was capable of producing returns of 10 percent or more guaranteed until you reached normal retirement age according to the Social Security Administration, and in my twenty years in the financial services industry, I can't recall any of these opportunities.

So if we follow the math, it's better to hold off receiving Social Security as long as you can, but it is a personal decision for everyone. Not everyone may have the means to hold off. If the income would make a difference in your life now and could get you closer to realizing some of your retirement dreams, then by all means, begin taking Social Security when it's in the best interest of you, not the math.

The problem with Social Security is once you've started the process, you can't go back. It's a one time only decision and a very hard decision to make. Many retirees who are able to work a few more years choose to do so in order to hold off on receiving benefits until age 66 and 70. If you're sick of working and you have assets that could supplement the income to your household, then taking benefits may not be a problem for you, but just remember that up until you reach normal retirement age of 65 or 66, Social Security will tax your benefits $1 for every $2 you make in income over the allowable limit. This is a very sore spot for retirees.

Applying for Your Benefits

The time to apply for your Social Security benefits is about three to four months prior to your eligibility. There are a number of ways to apply and all are convenient. You may call 1-800-772-1213 and a representative from the Social Security Administration will make an appointment for your application information to be taken over the phone or at a local Social Security office. If you're comfortable using the internet you can also apply online by going to www.ssa.gov. By going online, this could save you from making a trip to the local office and waiting in lines to discuss your impending benefits.

Whichever method you choose to use to begin the application process, you will be required to provide information to verify you are who you say you are. This information includes:

- Date of Birth
- Social Security Number
- W-2 forms or self employment tax return for the past year.
- Military discharge papers if you served.
- Proof of U.S. citizenship or lawful alien status if you were not born in the United States.
- Name of Bank and your account number so your benefits may be directly deposited into your account.

Once you've provided this information and completed your application, you will be well on your way to receiving benefits for which you've been paying in for so long.

Medicare

During most of your working years, you probably didn't have to concern yourself with finding health coverage for you and your family. In many cases you or your spouses' employment provided health coverage for your family, and the premium was taken from your paycheck every month.

In today's world, many retirees are losing the benefit of remaining under their company's health coverage once they are retired. The spiraling costs of healthcare have forced many companies to eliminate retiree health plans, leaving retirees searching for a replacement until Medicare becomes available. According to a Kaiser Family Foundation study in March 2004, Americans over age 65 will spend approximately 22 percent of their disposable income on healthcare costs, compared with only 11 percent in 1970.

Medicare was originally created to help bridge the cap of taking care of working Americans who could not afford, or could not be covered under insurance plans, but as life expectancy has increased and healthcare costs have skyrocketed, Medicare is now being relied upon to cover millions of aging Americans, something it was never intended to provide.

In 2006 Medicare was divided into 3 key parts: Part A, Part B, and Part D. Medicare Part A covers inpatient hospital, skilled nursing facility, home health, and hospice services. Medicare Part B covers almost all reasonable and necessary medical services including physician services, outpatient hospital care, durable medical equipment, lab tests, x-rays, therapy, mental health assistance, and ambulance services. Most retirees are familiar with these services provided by the government. Medicare Part D is the new outpatient prescription drug benefit available only through Medicare private drug plans or Medicare private health plans. Visit www.medicare.gov/publications for the most up to date information regarding your Medicare benefits.

If you've decided to accept your Social Security early and you're already enrolled, your Medicare enrollment is automatic when you turn sixty-five. However, you should contact Social Security and verify your coverage is in place.

If you have decided to defer your Social Security payments, you are able to enroll for Medicare with the Social Security office during a seven month period beginning three months before your 65th birthday. You may also enroll between January 1 and March 31 of any year after you become eligible, but you may have to pay a penalty for late enrollment. If you apply during this period, your Medicare coverage will not start until July 1 of the year in wish you enroll, so, the point of the matter is to be proactive and take advantage of this government service while it's fresh in your mind.

If you or your spouse has coverage under an employer health plan, you are able to enroll in Medicare at any time while you are covered under the health plan. If you or your spouse end your health plan coverage, or you stop working, you have a special eight month enrollment period beginning when you lose your coverage or stop working, whichever comes first. If you still receive coverage from your former employer as a retiree, it is considered retiree coverage and pays after Medicare pays, so it's important to sign up for Medicare anyway in order to cover your expenses.

Medicare covers reasonable and necessary health care costs. In 2006 Medicare will begin to cover a small portion of outpatient prescription drugs as well, but it will not cover routine checkups, dental services, custodial or long term nursing home care, experimental procedures which are often found in cancer treatments, and most prescription drug costs. In order to limit prescription drug costs, you should consider choosing the Medicare D coverage that is suitable for you and your family when you are eligible to enroll in Medicare. More information on the Medicare prescription plan may be found by going to www.medicare.gov.

Coverage Issues

Once you qualify for Medicare, it should cover most health care issues that you or your doctor feel you need. If you get a service and Medicare denies coverage, you can challenge the denial through an appeals process. Consult with your state Social Security office for more information.

Most doctors will accept Medicare patients, but more and more doctors are choosing private insurance over Medicare due to escalating costs and lower payments back to the doctors. Before you sign on with a doctor, make sure that he will accept Medicare. The last thing you would want is to search for a new doctor who is not up to date of the quality of care you've been receiving.

On December 31, 2005, Medicare recipients became eligible for prescription drug coverage through Medicare D. While the government provides the ability for citizens to receive Medical coverage that covers most of their healthcare needs under Medicare A & B, the cost of preventative medicine has placed a huge burden on retiree budgets. Medicare D now offers retirees the opportunity to have a large portion of their prescription drug costs paid for through Medicare. It's possible the company you retired from may offer prescription drug coverage, but visit the Medicare site in order to determine which plan is best suited for you. You may be surprised by the cost savings provided by the Medicare D plan.

Once you reach Medicare, it doesn't necessarily mean you can stop budgeting. While Medicare will pick up a large portion of your health care costs, it does not cover all the costs. There will be a co-payment and deductibles you must meet on a monthly basis under the Medicare laws. Just as you had to expense certain items as you raised your family such as a mortgage, car payment, college tuition, or clothing funds, you need budget for these healthcare costs.

If you retire before 65, it's likely you will pay for all your health insurance coverage unless you were lucky enough to work for a company that continued to offer you health coverage until you became Medicare eligible. If your company does not offer coverage, it may serve in your best interest to wait until 18 months before your 65th birthday to retire so that you can take advantage of COBRA benefits. COBRA is the federal law that says you may buy up to eighteen additional months of health insurance from your former employer (usually at a higher premium, but less than purchasing private insurance). In order to avoid any coverage issues, you need to retire after you've worked a thousand or more hours for the year, usually around July 1, or the extra 18 months of available health insurance will start as of December 31 of whatever year you last worked that long which is often the year before.

If you choose to retire prior to 18 months prior to age 65 and you need private insurance to cover yourself and your family, it is likely that many companies will require physicals on you and anyone else within your family that you wish to cover. The added cost for private insurance, depending on your health and prior conditions, could run very high, making it almost cost prohibitive to own. So before you tell your boss to "take this job and shove it", research available private insurance quotes and determine whether waiting until age 63 1/2 may be in your best interest financially. For more information on COBRA, visit www.dol.gov and search COBRA.

Filling the "Gap"

As healthcare costs continue to escalate it's important that you consider some type of *Medigap* insurance coverage to help you with the added expense of covering your healthcare and prescription costs. Whether this is through the Federal Government (see www.medicare.gov for more information or call 1-800-772-1213) or your own private insurance, it's a budgetary item that needs to be included in your budget and adjusted for inflationary pressures each and every year.

Medigap is a supplemental insurance policy that provided by private insurers which cover services and visits to doctors that Medicare A or B may not cover, but generally it is used to cover Medicare's coinsurance, co-payments, and deductibles that Medicare A and B do not cover. There are typically 10 types labeled A–J. They all provide basic benefits, such as Medicare A coinsurance and hospital benefits, Medicare B coinsurance and co-payments, and three pints of blood per calendar year. But A provides the least coverage and costs least, while J provides the most coverage and costs the most.

In order to determine which policy is best for you depends on your current health and family history. If you have a chronic condition that is likely to require skilled home health care in the future, you've had a serious illness that may require extensive outpatient treatment, or you want to know that you will be cared for in the future, you should consider the more expensive plans that cover both skilled nursing and home recovery. Conversely if you have had routine check ups and your health has remained good throughout your working life, you may choose to accept coverage that provides hospital, doctor, and prescription services.

Cost will play a large role in the determine what form of Medigap coverage you choose which explains why it is necessary to account for these costs in your household budget, but while cost may be an issue, you will never have to worry about whether you will be able to receive coverage. A resource you can turn to for more information on your rights under Medicare is the Medicare Rights Center. The Medicare Rights Center is an independent source of healthcare information that provides a free e-newsletter at www.medicarerights.org.

When you retire and you've qualified for Medicare coverage, you basically have one opportunity to get insurance when insurance companies are prohibited from turning you down for health reasons or preexisting conditions. It's the open enrollment period that begins when you enroll in Medicare B (which provides physician services) and lasts for six months. If you enroll during this window, insurance companies can't change the coverage they offer or charge higher premiums, so don't procrastinate.

Another form of Medicare is the Medicare Advantage Plan that is available to retirees over the age of sixty-five. This type of coverage allows you to utilize HMO's, PPO's, and PFFS. This plan may offer lower out of pocket costs to you. In some situations the Medicare HMO will solicit you for your business by sending you letters that tell you they can substantially reduce your medical and insurance expenses when you join their HMO since you won't need Medigap insurance. This may be true, but be aware that once you join these organizations, access to medical care will be limited only to the doctors in their network and access to specialists may require a referral from your HMO primary doctor. Many HMO's have been under financial pressure and have reduced benefits, raised rates, or both. Other providers and doctors have gotten out of the Medicare business. If this happens to a Medicare HMO you belong to, you must choose a new doctor and start a new relationship or enroll in Medicare and purchase a Medigap policy.

When it comes to Medicare's drug coverage, the current plan is designed to cap the annual amount any person over 65 pays for prescriptions. Participation is optional. You can't be denied coverage for health reasons. It is a subsidized plan offered by the government, but you are responsible for paying a portion of the cost. The plan is sold by private insurers and there are a variety of policies to choose from.

Once you turn 65 information on the available plans will be sent to you. Once again you will need to consider which plan is best for you based upon your current health. If you're not certain, you can contact the Medicare toll free number or visit the Medicare website for more information at www.medicare.gov.

What You Should Consider When Choosing Medicare Coverage

1. Cost—Understand what you will pay out of pocket including premiums.

2. Benefits—Are the extra benefits and services such as additional drug coverage, eye exams, hearing aids, or annual physicals covered under the plan?

3. Doctors and Hospitals—Can you see the doctor(s) you want to see? Do you need a referral to see a specialist? Can you go to the hospital of your choosing?

4. Convenience—Where are the doctors' offices located? What are their hours? Does their office offer accessibility when you need it? Are they accepting new patients? Can they refer you to another doctor in another state?

5. Prescription drugs—Are they covered under the plan you are considering? Are your prescription drugs on the plan's list of covered drugs?

6. Pharmacy—Can you use the pharmacy of your choice?

7. Quality of Care—How is the quality of care of the plans in the area?

As you consider companies that will provide Medigap insurance, be mindful of policies that seem too good to be true. Many of these types of policies may have restrictive provisions which could make it impossible to receive benefits from the insurer. If you are in the market to purchase a Medigap policy, it may be well worth the $49 dollars to purchase a report from the Weiss Ratings.

The Weiss Ratings is an independent company which provides reviews based upon several financial instruments in today's marketplace including Medigap insurance. The Weiss Ratings Company is the only major rating agency that receives no direct or indirect compensation from the companies they rate. For $49, they will provide you with a list of Medigap insurance plans and providers in your area, tailored to your needs. You can review the ratings for all the insurance companies you may be considering by visiting their website at www.weissratings.com or by calling them toll free at 1-800-289-9222. The small investment you make to acquire their research could save you hundreds or thousands of dollars in the future.

The Weiss Ratings avoid companies which require you to join an organization, pay dues, or promises to insure everyone in your household regardless of their health. If a company requests a large up front payment to enter the plan or does not provide any type of plan documents about the plan, you should consider another company.

If you already have health problems that prevent you from purchasing insurance direct from a commercial insurance company, your state may have a high-risk insurance pool for people like you, enabling you to get coverage. More than half the states have such pools, and while the premiums are usually higher than for individual coverage, they might be your only choice, and can sometimes even be fairly economical.

Your state may offer other cost-saving programs, too. Contact your state's Health Insurance Assistance Program for information (call 800-633-4227 toll-free to find out the phone number of the office in your state).

Potential Changes Social Security and Medicare Benefits

Social Security will affect every retiree in the future. Understanding your benefits could have a direct impact on your Personal Retirement Road Map now and in the future. As our government continues to look for ways to care for its retirees, it's likely that laws governing Medicare and Social Security could change in the near future. It's important to stay alert of impending changes that could affect you and your family. Consult the government's website for more information at www.ssa.gov and www.medicare.gov.

There are several resources you may turn to which can keep you abreast of potential changes and current laws. You could consult the government's website for more information at www.ssa.gov or www.medicare.gov. If you can't find the information you're looking for or you need further clarification, visit your local Social Security office and speak with an agent who can explain your benefits in more detail.

Another resource you can turn to is AARP. As we mentioned before, AARP is a valuable resource for many retirees and soon to be retirees. The information they offer concerning Social Security benefits, Medicare, and Medigap insurance could answer many questions asked by many retirees today. Their Medigap site, which contains a nice five-step guide to finding Medi-gap coverage, is www.aarp.org/health/medicare/supplemental.

If you have questions with regards to rights under the Medicare program, you may visit the Center for Medicare Advocacy, at www.medicareadvocacy.org/FAQMedigap.htm and the Medicare Rights Center at www.medicarerights.org for more information. This resource provides detailed information as to the rights you have under the law.

Social Security and Medicare will play a large role in retirement. In some cases it will determine when you retire, when you can retire, and when you will begin receiving benefits. The benefits you and your family receive during retirement could determine how many of your retirement dreams will become a reality. Please give it the attention it deserves. Take time to research all the benefits you are entitled to and rely upon professionals to help you make the appropriate decision as it relates to your personal needs.

8

Allocating Assets in Retirement

According to Webster's, asset allocation by definition is: *the process of dividing investments among different kinds or assets such as stocks, bonds, real estate, and cash to optimize the risk/reward tradeoff based on an individual's or institution's specific situation and goals.* While this may be the definition, it is anything but clear.

I describe asset allocation to retirees I work with as the process in determining the best way to allocate or invest assets you own in order to realize an acceptable rate of return according to your tolerance towards risk. What is considered an acceptable rate of return is different for everyone, so too is their attitude towards risk.

There are other factors I include in my definition of asset allocation where Webster's does not and these are TIME and MONEY. It's important to know how much TIME you anticipate spending in retirement and the amount of MONEY you will have available to invest. What many retirees will find out is that their retirement may be as long as thirty years, but they may not have enough money to last through retirement.

Unfortunately there's no formula today which can tell you the exact asset allocation you should take as it relates to investing your assets. Asset allocation is different for everyone. Over the years financial planners and advisors have recommended asset allocation based upon a person's age. A retiree age 60 would allocate 60 percent of their investable assets into investments which offered stability of principle and income such as c.d.'s, bonds, or money markets. The theory was that these assets would likely be needed as the investor grew older, thus stability of principle would be very important. The remainder should be allocated in investments which have exposure to the equity markets.

Allocating Assets in Retirement

T. Rowe Price, a well-known mutual fund company, recently suggested the ideal asset allocation for a retiree should consist of 60 percent of their investable assets in the stock markets and the remainder in investments which offered a fixed income. The T. Rowe Price study used statistical information based upon historical market cycles.

The following tables forecast the probability of having enough assets to last through retirement. These tables provide guidelines with regards to various factors that could effect your retirement including the estimated time period you will need to rely on the funds, the amount of pretax withdrawal you anticipate taking, and the asset allocation of your funds. These tables assume pretax withdrawals from tax deferred accounts and may be applied towards any portfolio size.

20 Year Retirement Period

Withdrawal Amount	Stock/Bond Allocation			
	80/20	60/40	40/60	20/80
>7%	56%	52%	44%	26%
>6%	74%	75%	75%	71%
>5%	89%	92%	95%	97%
>4%	97%	99%	99%	99%

25 Year Retirement Period

Withdrawal Amount	Stock/Bond Allocation			
	80/20	60/40	40/60	20/80
>7%	39%	30%	17%	4%
>6%	57%	53%	44%	25%
>5%	77%	78%	78%	73%
>4%	91%	94%	97%	98%

30 Year Retirement Period

Withdrawal Amount	Stock/Bond Allocation			
	80/20	60/40	40/60	20/80

30 Year Retirement Period				
>7%	28%	19%	7%	1%
>6%	45%	38%	24%	7%
>5%	65%	63%	57%	40%
>4%	84%	87%	89%	89%

*The following asset allocations include short term bonds: 60/40 includes 60% stocks, 30% intermediate bonds (5–15 years), 10% short term bonds (0–5 years); 40/60 includes 40% stocks, 40% intermediate bonds, 20% short term bonds' 20/80 includes 20% stocks, 50% intermediate bonds, 30% short term bonds. The withdrawal rate is percentage of portfolio withdrawn the first year. That dollar amount is increased by 3% per year for cost of living adjustments. Probabilities are based on computerized simulations of historical performance of the S&P 500 and the appropriate 10 year and 2 year government bonds over many decades.

Source: T Rowe Price

The information assumes something that many investors fail to think about which is the cost of inflation in our world. Inflation is a cancer, just like taxes, which can eat away at the purchasing power of your investments. Consider a 65 year old married couple just entering retirement. In order to ensure they will have enough money to outlive them, their best probability of success is to invest 60 percent of their assets in the equity markets and the remainder in investments which provide stability of principle and interest. If they withdraw 4 percent from their assets, adjusted for inflation, it could provide them with the best percentage for success.

Another approach recommended more than a decade ago by William Bengen in a critically acclaimed study that was published in the Journal of Financial Planning, suggested that if a retiree would like to outlive his money, indexed for inflation, then a minimum of 50 percent of his assets needs to be invested in the equity markets, regardless of their age, and the maximum withdrawal they should pull from the nest egg would be 4 percent indexed for inflation each year. According to Mr. Bengen's analysis, this would guarantee that retirees would have enough assets to last them through retirement.

Mr. Bengen's original study was considered as such a breakthrough that the Journal reprinted the study in its March 2004 issue in celebration of the publications 25th anniversary. You can read the study in detail by visiting the magazines website online archives at: http://www.fpanet.org/journal/articles/2004_Issues/jfp0304-art8.cfm

Many retirees feel that once they reach retirement the growing of their assets isn't as important as the preservation and the income provided by their assets. The information from T. Rowe Price and Mr. Bengen suggest otherwise. Over the next thirty years retirees will see the cost of goods and services continue to rise and it's important that have some form of growth from their investments in order to compensate for these higher prices in the future.

To put percentages into numbers, consider the following scenario: A retiree has chosen to invest in a 5 percent c.d. for 10 years for his savings account and retirement account. He has a total of $200,000 which represents his nest egg. His need for additional retirement income is only $10,000 per year.

Each year his inflation costs increased nearly 5 percent (Inflation for retirees is usually higher due to health care and prescription costs). Based upon this information, he would determine that he should be withdrawing 5 ¼ percent next year from his investments versus 5 percent the current year. This equation is determined by multiplying the anticipated withdrawal rate times the inflation rate and adding it to the withdrawal rate from the previous year (5% X 5% +5%=Withdrawal Percentage), so it can be determined that next years income payment of $10,000 will not be enough to cover the inflationary cost of living.

If the retiree chooses to a 5 percent return over exposing his nest egg to growth, during the next ten years it's likely he will need to invade his nest egg to maintain his standard of living or cut back on his choices. Neither of these are scenarios that any retiree really wants to envision.

As you consider the proper asset allocation mix for your investments, make assumptions as to the anticipated rate of return you can expect from your assets. Include inflation estimates from your community within your Personal Retirement Road Map to see if your money would outlive you over a thirty year period. Don't worry about invading principle, but don't assume your investments will produce a 10 percent return.

There are too many occasions when investors and retirees alike become too aggressive or passive as it relates to their nest egg. These investors realize they won't have enough to last them through retirement and invest aggressively. If you retired in 2000 and followed the course of action during this period to invest all of your nest egg in the stock market, it's likely that serious damage took place and you may be back at work.

On the other hand if you choose to stay with c.d.'s and savings accounts, the cost of inflation alone could eat away at nearly 50 percent of your purchasing power in just ten years as you need to invade principle in order to maintain your standard of living.

Volatile markets and reduced purchasing power are options that retirees would love to avoid, but if history is any gauge they are likely to continue. Retirees will need to balance their assets and the best balance may be an asset allocation of 50 percent equities and 50 percent fixed income. Review your asset allocation every six months, primary near the beginning of May and November (more discussion as to why this period is better in Chapter13: Beating the Markets). If the equity percentage of your allocation has grown above 50 percent, skim a percentage of these profits and invest in fixed income assets which provide stability of principle and income. If the occasion arises that you need to skim from the investments that offer stability of principle and interest, and invest these assets in the market, don't worry about the markets. It may simply represent an opportunity to buy low today and sell high six months from now. If you follow this strategy, your investment portfolio should show a smoother growing progression over time which builds confidence and relives stress over you investments.

Think about it this way. When you buy new tires for your car, you've made a sizable investment. Do you have them balanced? Do you rotate them? Of course you do because you realize that as long as you've made an investment in your car; your investment could go much farther by making minor adjustments over time. It's no different in asset allocation.

Remember you are on a journey towards your dreams and goals. Everyone is starting their journey from a different point in their life, but no one can stay on the road forever without a break. During these breaks such as market events, a significant birthday, and at least twice a year, you'll need to take a break and review your Personal Retirement Road Map to not only ensure that you're progressing towards your dreams and goals, but that your retirement assets are properly allocated based upon your risk tolerance, the amount of time you have remaining in retirement and the amount of money you will need in retirement.

9

Get in Touch with your Emotions

> *"We simply attempt to be fearful when others are greedy and to be greedy only when others are fearful."*
>
> —*Warren Buffet*

The Oracle of Omaha, Warren Buffet has made millions for others while making billions for himself by following an investment philosophy learned many years ago by Benjamin Graham, a noted investor and mentor to Warren Buffet. Benjamin Graham often tutored his disciples such as Warren Buffet to follow 3 key rules when it came to investing.

1. True investors are calm.

They understand that prices rise and fall. As long as the company retains the qualities that encouraged the investment, the value will go back up. On the other side, a true investor is not affected by the "mob influence." When everyone is making the same choices, no one is in a position to profit. True investors don't worry about missing the party. They worry about coming to the party not dressed for the occasion.

2. True investors are patient.

They will say "no" more often than they will say "yes". They avoid being swept into the enthusiasm of the crowd. One great perspective is to evaluate every opportunity as if you have only 20 investment decisions to make your entire life. If an investor's emotions were restrained in this way, they would be forced to wait patiently until a great investment opportunity presents itself.

3. True investors are rational.

Neither unduly optimistic, nor unduly pessimistic, an investor uses rational and logical thinking to determine investment strategy. The emotional investor typically feels optimistic when the market is rising and pessimistic when the market is in decline. In so many cases these emotions influence an emotional investor to sell at lower price and buy at higher price, which is not the best strategy to generate profits. The true investor realizes that while irrational optimism creates unduly high prices, irrational pessimism creates bargains.

Warren Buffet has followed these 3 rules for more than 40 years and over that time, he has seen the share value of Berkshire Hathaway (BRK—New York Stock Exchange), the publicly traded company where he is the Chief Executive Officer, rise from $1,000 per share to more than $100,000 per share today. Warren's secret has been his ability to understand and control two key emotions which wreaks havoc in nearly every retiree's life today, *greed* and *fear*. This is not to say that he does not make mistakes along the way, he does, and he has, but he puts these mistakes behind him and learns from his experience.

There is no way during any given day or cycle you can predict exactly what the markets will do, but if you have confidence in your Personal Retirement Road Map and understand that detours will occur due to unforeseen events, the experience you gain should help you avoid these hazards in the future.

True Investors are Calm

When adversity slaps you in the face do you remain calm or do you over react? Remember 9–11, what was your reaction regarding your investments at that time? Were you losing sleep until the markets were ready to reopen again a week later or were you planning a strategy to take advantage of the weakness? Turbulent times such as 9–11 and the recession that followed will always be a part of our lives and shape the investment landscape. What will be more important are your actions during these events. Will you play Chicken Little or will you look for opportunities like Warren?

Let me share with you a real life experience of Pat and Cheryl Lansing. Pat and Cheryl have been owners of one of the more successful fence companies in Orlando, Florida. In October of 1999 they sold their fence company and made a decision to invest the assets with several mutual fund managers who had outstanding performance over the past few years.

In March of 2000 as the markets reached all time highs, they had seen the value of their investments rise nearly fifty percent. They were giddy. They purchased a new boat, purchased a vacation property, and gave money to their children. They were so pleased with the value of some of their mutual funds; they sold some of the lower returning funds and reallocated these assets into the technology mutual funds which had done so well.

During the year the markets had been volatile, but each time the markets sold off, they regained their traction. To Pat and Cheryl, this represented an opportunity for them to reallocate more money into the tech mutual funds in order to buy these funds at an even lower price.

By February 2001, Pat and Cheryl began to get a bit uneasy with the fall out of their tech mutual funds. Their portfolio which had done so well had now fallen well below their original investment. They continued to reallocate their portfolio until all their money was invested in the tech fund. In their eyes, the tech fund would represent the best opportunity to get their money back quickly, and then came 9–11.

The inability to successfully predict what the markets will do from one day to the next is why there is risk in the markets. Pat and Cheryl didn't have a plan in place and were following the recommendations of the media, magazines, and friends. They didn't want to admit that they had allowed their emotions to get the best of them. They had encountered greed and fear all within the span of under two years. In essence, they allowed their emotions to get the best of them.

Market events will always occur. Some of these events will be bad and some will be good. What's important is that you evaluate the current environment and ask yourself, 'how can I benefit from this event or situation?' If you can adopt this forward way of thinking, it will not only provide you with confidence you can rely upon in future years to make investment decisions, but it could help with keeping your emotions in check.

As we discussed in the previous chapter, as the markets present emotions of euphoria as the Dow nears highs, or fear as the Dow nears low, this is an ideal time to review your asset allocation. Rely upon Personal Retirement Road Map as your guide to reallocate your assets when events occur such as market downturns or euphoric new highs, and when you make these changes, continue to look forward towards your goal.

There is nothing you can do to change the past. Too many investors sell a fund or stock only to see it continue to move higher. If you continue to look back at these decisions, you could find yourself in a position you rely on past experiences to make your decisions, not based upon you're your Road Map is telling you. Understand when you make changes to your investments, it is in the best interest of your long term financial goals. What happens after these changes is immaterial and in the past. Warren Buffet may have regretted selling some of these positions, but he never looked back. He realizes there will always be an opportunity ahead of him.

True Investors are Patient

As a society our tendency is to *want it now*. It really doesn't matter what "it" is. We just know we want "it" now. When it comes to investing, long term investors who follow a game plan and invest with managers who have a long term perspective have historically outperformed the day traders and nervous investors according to a recent Dalbar study.

The study also stated that most investors invariably buy **high** and sell **low.** It also suggested that many of these same type of *want it now* investors choose to buy the best performing mutual fund when a financial magazine focuses on "*The Best Funds to Own in 2020*" versus asking the question, how does this funds performance help me reach my financial and retirement goals?

As funds don't perform based upon investors' expectations, they may choose to sell quickly due to their greedy expectations or hold their investment at a loss in order to save face. Whatever the result, these decisions tend to become bad habits over time. The more an investor buys and sells mutual funds or makes changes to his overall investments, the lower the expected return. It doesn't matter if these investors invest in stocks, bonds, or real estate. What the study points out is that the investor who decided to buy and hold his investment for a period of 10 years outperformed the average speculative investor by more than 3 to 1.

No one knows where the markets will take us from one day to the next, but it's important that we at least monitor all aspects of your Personal Retirement Road Map in order to assure that funds will be available when you need them. Warren Buffet didn't become rich overnight, but he did follow a methodology and a plan that created wealth over time during all market conditions.

While Warren is patient, it doesn't mean that he doesn't review his holdings. His review of his holdings will likely be much different from yours. It's a bit different when you have more than fifty billion dollars in assets.

The review of your Personal Retirement Road Map will be just as important as the preparation of the map itself. What good is it if you bought a map of Orlando, Florida, in 1965 and you're taking a trip in 1976? Do you think things may have changed during that period?

My experience has told me the best opportunity to review your Personal Retirement Road Map is every six months and during extreme market volatility. Reviewing your Road Map during these occasions should allow you to see if adjustments should be made with regards towards your investments, skimming profits from some areas and reallocating into other areas that may not have performed as well.

A mistake that many retirees make is they take the time to create a "financial plan", but they don't take the time to monitor the plan and make adjustments along the way. Those who do take the time to review their plan, usually review their plan once a year, and usually at the end of the year.

I prefer to review plans every six months. The first is after tax season and the second is prior to Thanksgiving. These reviews make practical sense for many reasons. Retirees may need to write a check to the IRS during the month of April and this is a great time to review your assets and determine which assets will be used to pay taxes. November is a great time to review your progress on your Personal Retirement Road Map prior to visiting family for the holidays or considering gifts at the end of the year.

But there is another reason I recommend retirees review their Road Map during *early* May and November. A chapter in this book is dedicated to discussing the seasonality of the markets and why April and November represent the best opportunities to review your investments (*Chapter 13 Beating the Markets*). It will shed more light on market seasonality and why these periods provide opportunities to shift your investment portfolio.

Review your Road Map is to ease your emotions. These reviews not only allow you an opportunity to review your dreams and goals, but provide an opportunity to make minor adjustments during periods of extreme volatility. Use this time to review the performance of your investments and determine if your asset allocation plan is out of balance. By making these minor adjustments when these opportunities present themselves, you will find yourself avoiding other periods that could be more damaging to your investments.

True Investors are Rational

There are so many uncertainties in life which affect retirees, the last thing you need is to see your nest egg fall apart during market events. It's likely you've spent the better part of your working life investing in 401(k) and retirement accounts. These assets were likely invested in mutual funds which provided the opportunity for growth. Over time your assets have built up to a position where you may feel comfortable taking the retirement jump, but now it's up to you to protect the nest. You won't be making contributions into your accounts anymore and the volatility within the markets will likely create emotions that could cause you to make decisions at a time that may not be in your best interest. What is important is you understand that you will have these emotions and have a plan in place to deal with them when they occur. In essence, it's important to be rational.

Investment returns are far more dependent on investor behavior than the performance of the investment. Unfortunately not every investor has been as successful as Warren Buffet or Benjamin Graham. Most investors have historically made bad decisions under the pressure and stress of trying to beat the markets. These shortfalls are directly attributed to their overreactions to constantly changing conditions in financial markets, where they have absolutely no control. The tendency has been for investors to bail out of stock funds during market downturns and buy back after a period of time has gone by to indicate its "safe" to get back in. The problem with this strategy is that just when they think it's safe to drink the water, most of the water is gone.

Remember the talk that used to take place at work or at parties in the late 90's where people were bragging on an initial public offering or the tech stock they bought that doubled in a day. These stories were abundant as it encouraged many people, like Pat and Cheryl who had no business investing in individual stocks or aggressive stock funds, to invest all their retirement savings and nest eggs into tech funds or aggressive small cap stock funds. While the returns for the short term may have been impressive, *greed* continued to have investors thinking their stock would return to their original purchase price, only to sell the position in 2002 when the markets reached an ultimate bottom. In many cases these decisions were based on their *fear* of losing more.

There is a difference between investing and speculating. The stock markets have historically moved in cycles. Depending on what time you may have entered a cycle could have a dramatic impact on your overall investment results. Stocks have had their period of speculating, so has real estate, oil drilling and gold bullion.

As you consider making an investment, it's important to understand how this specific investment will get you closer to your retirement dreams and goals. What purpose will these assets serve in the future? How long are you willing to let these investments run their course? What is your exit strategy should your situation or market conditions change? Many investors especially retirees, have made mistakes by changing how they invest in retirement because they realize they need more from their assets than what their assets may be able to provide. While they may understand the volatile nature of the markets, they lack the necessary patience needed to make the investment.

It's so important to make rational investment decisions based upon your past investment history and are driven from a plan such as your Personal Retirement Road Map. By having a plan in place, investment decisions are based upon the best route to for you based upon facts, not emotions. Your Personal Retirement Road Map can help you to make the right investment decisions at the right time and ultimately provide you with confidence in knowing the plan you have in place is working for you regardless of market turmoil.

Information Overload

There are plenty of opinions as it relates to the investment world. These days retired investors have thousands of resources they can turn to collect information and opinions about the markets. Unfortunately, as they gather this information, it may become overwhelming or confusing.

If you remember anything about this section, remember this, the role of the media is to SELL. It doesn't matter if it's magazines, newspapers, or commercials. All media is designed to create a shock value which is designed to grab your attention. It doesn't matter if the information is good or bad. The intent is to create interest and increase advertising.

Think about the last time you visited an airport magazine shop. Which financial magazine would you pick up first, *"Why the Markets Will Fall 30% This Year"* or *"The Fixing of General Motors"*?

If you're honest, you would pick up the first one because it appears more pressing. Right?

Many of the mainstream media are trying to draw a reaction from you so you will tune into their show, visit their website, or buy their magazine or newspaper. The media today is about shock value. The greater the shock value, the greater the opportunity to sell, or at the very least, use your purchase as a way to increase the cost to advertisers.

Over the years I've consistently told my clients that some of the best investment opportunities have been made when certain "events" took place and CNBC concentrated on the doom and gloom in the markets. A few examples of these periods included August 1998 (Long Term Capital Hedge Fund Crisis), October 1998 (Chinese Economic Crisis), 9–11, October 2002(3rd quarter GDP shows negative Growth for the U.S. Economy), March 2003 (Iraq Invasion). When these "events" occur, investor's emotions get the best of them as they react to the news. While they should be buying low, many are going into shelter mode waiting for the next shoe to drop, but history points out, and history is a very powerful tool you should rely on, in everyone of these instances in time, it represented one of the best buying opportunities for investors, but yet, most did nothing or sold positions and invested in money markets and c.d.'s, exactly the opposite of what Warren Buffet would have done.

The media wants to use whatever the market gives them in order to create interest with viewers. They are going to provide the best in entertainment and contributors that money can buy in order to reap higher advertising sales from their customers.

So before you consider selling all your investments and buying gold coins because of a radio ad caught your attention, you may want to consider Warren Buffet's philosophy of going the opposite way when you see the dust coming your way, in essence, don't follow the herd, run from it.

The markets will continue to have "events" along the way and the media will continue to exploit them. What is important is that you understand that these events will take place, and react by revisiting your Personal Retirement Road Map to see how these events have affected your investments, and what you can do to take advantage of the opportunities they present. If you follow this methodology, you will be well on your way to controlling your emotions and enjoying your retirement years.

10

Obstacles to Avoid

You've had to deal with so many uncertainties most of your adult life. Now that your at or nearing retirement it's nice to know that you should be able to rely on Social Security and Medicare benefits, but these contributors can only get you so far. Most retirees will find it necessary to depend on their investments, savings, and other retirement income to help maintain their standard of living during retirement, but even these benefits will face obstacles that may not be obvious.

Market volatility and how you handle your emotions will play a large role in determining your retirement future. These are conditions you can prepare for based upon your actions, but there are other less obvious obstacles you will face in retirement that could be equally devastating to your dreams and goals.

These are important areas retirees should not take for granted when it comes to managing their assets during retirement.

1.Depending on Steady Returns

There can only be one Warren Buffet and many of us lack the golden touch when it comes to making investment purchases. I can't recall when I heard it, but I do recall a time when a money manager once said he needed only 3 stocks of every 10 in his portfolio to produce positive returns. At that time, I thought to myself, anyone could do that, but invariably the 3 stocks I thought would be *winners* didn't perform as I would have liked.

How many times did you actually make an investment and anticipate it going up immediately after you purchased it? It's likely you checked the paper or contacted your broker every day to see where the stock was trading at the time. You anticipated it trading higher only to see it drop immediately after its purchase.

This wasn't anything to lose sleep over at the time, but it's likely you questioned your purchase.

Investors who rely on the past performance of the markets or mutual funds to determine the distribution amount they can safely pull from their retirement assets, and assume their retirement assets will remain the same or grow in value, are likely heading down a path of disappointment. It's true that over time the equity markets have produced double digit returns for investors, but this is not done consistently. There are times, such as 2000–2005 when the markets destroyed many investment portfolios and retirement dreams. The expectations were for the market to return to *normality* within a very short period of time, but as we learned earlier, the emotion of fear can be just as powerful as the emotion of greed, especially as you watch retirement assets lose value on a daily basis. If you assume that your assets will provide steady returns year after year, you're either very lucky or are wishful thinking, either way, it's important to understand that the markets do not go in one direction.

Sometimes there are detours along the way which create new experiences, some good such as 1995 to 2000 and some not so good such as 2000 to 2005. When you're IN retirement, a five year period of underperformance within the markets can devastate a retirement portfolio. This is especially true based upon the added risk you take when you select your investments.

Rather than depending on steady and consistent returns, you should rely upon your Personal Retirement Road Map to serve as your guide. If you simply wait for the markets or stocks to get back to levels you paid for them, it may be years before these assets get back to prices you paid, all the while other areas of the market may have performed better. By taking the time to review your Personal Retirement Road Map at least twice a year and especially during volatile market periods, you can get a snapshot of how your investments are performing, and hopefully take the appropriate action to maneuver your assets to take advantage of the volatile market conditions.

There are some investments available that have shown evidence of providing returns that have been more steady than most. As you consider the best investment options for you and your family, find those money managers or mutual fund manager or companies which performed well during difficult times. In many cases, these are companies or funds which provided a consistent dividend to their shareholders. These types of investments provide some stability to a portfolio during some very difficult decisions. As you consider these types of investments, you will get a better idea of managers who had success managing *real dollars* or a *real company* during very difficult times such as 2000 to 2002 when the markets were at their most volatile. For more information on these managers you can turn to companies who provide research on these managers such as Morningstar (www.morningstar.com) and Value Line (www.valueline.com).

2. That Sucking Sound is the Sound of Your Assets

No one knows when the next bull or bear market will strike, but retirees should act as if a grizzly has decided to make their backyard home. In the first few years of your retirement, it's likely you will find yourself pulling more income and assets from your investments as you take trips, fix the house, and take care of other odds and ends, but you really need to consider if some of these projects can be put off a few years especially as you determine whether you will have enough retirement income to meet your needs.

Retirees who need their investment and retirement assets to last two to three decades should consider drawing the least amount of income from their retirement assets in the first year of retirement. It's much easier to increase your standard of living if you have too much money than it is to cut back when you begin to run low.

If a retiree considered a 25 year retirement period and a withdrawal of just over 4 percent per year, adjusted for inflation, he could conclude he would have enough assets to last him through retirement, but if he decided to pull 6 percent from his investments over the same period of time, his probability of having enough money to last during retirement could reach as low as 25 percent. For this reason, it's much easier to have more later in life when health care costs could be high versus having much less when your health *care* is a concern.

In Mr. Bengen's analysis, his recommendation is that retirees should look to invest as much as their risk tolerance will allow them in stocks. His research points out those investments allocations below 50 percent in equities are counterproductive as the client is actually accepting an equal degree of risk for less reward. Of course this is predicated on the risk tolerance of the client, but he should be made aware that his assets are likely to be eliminated much sooner should he decide to choose a path of withdrawing a higher percentage of income and accept a lower degree of risk. The notion of investing 50 percent of your assets in the stock market may be a concern for many retirees, but over time, Mr. Bengen's analysis is correct, especially if you are counting on maintaining your current standard of living for years to come.

3. Don't Allow Fees to Influence Your Decision

Once again I'm left talking about many of these so called experts who typically write for newspapers or magazines and never had a real job where they had to rely upon commissions or sales for a living. While it's easy for them criticize with the power of the pen, what they fail to understand is the fees charged by many managers are justified and well worth the price paid.

No load funds are offered by mutual fund management companies which do not charge commissions to their investors. This is not to say the fund is free of expenses or fees, but in most cases, there is no cost to the investor to purchase the fund. If you invest $10,000, all of your investment goes to work the first day.

Conversely load funds charge investors a commission or sales charge. Depending on the fund, you could invest your $10,000 but only $9,500 is actually invested. The difference is usually shared between the investment advisor and the firm.

The popularity of *no load* funds has forced the *load* fund industry to change their commission structure. Investors don't appreciate watching the value of their account drop immediately after a purchase. This has forced many mutual fund companies to change their sales charge structure to compete with no load funds.

I can certainly understand how you want to be cost conscious during retirement, but are you content on eating at home every night during your retirement? Wouldn't it be nice to eat out once in a while at your favorite restaurant?

The availability of mutual fund managers today is simply astounding. Today, there are more mutual funds trading on the exchanges than there are stocks on the New York Stock Exchange.

Many managers who charge very low expenses and in their funds and have no upfront sales charges invest based upon modeling an index, thus a computer tells them what should be bought. In essence, you don't really need a manager. The question then is, would you rather have a manager actively managing your funds or a computer?

Investing is so much more than what a computer may recommend. Today many pension funds are choosing to allocate assets with these low cost managers in order to offer "value" to their participants, but as more and more money is allocated towards these funds, it makes it more difficult for these funds to reduce the positions they hold and their performance can suffer.

The best manager to hire would be a manager who charges an acceptable fee relative to his overall return. To find out which managers provide this ability you could visit www.morningstar.com or meet with your financial advisor to determine which funds are best for you.

If you want to determine if you should pay a fee for the management of your assets, consider this question: Would you be willing to pay someone 1 ½ percent if they consistently provided you with a 13 percent return over the past five years (in essence doubling your return)? Or would you feel better earning an 8 percent return from a manager who has minimal expenses return over the same period?

A benefit you may not realize is that many no load managers could have a higher degree of volatility and taxable events within their portfolio than a load fund. According to a study by the Mutual Fund Education Alliance, no load funds have shown a tendency to have a greater amount of volatility than no load funds. One of the primary reasons for this is the ease in which investors can sell their fund on any days notice when their emotions overtake them. No load fund managers are not set up to advise investors on their decision and thus when they make the decision to sell, they liquidate their fund. If enough investors choose to sell, especially during volatile times, or buy during euphoric times, it could impact their performance dramatically.

Conversely, retirees who work with financial professionals who recommended a fund based upon the clients risk tolerance and investment objective, these managers found themselves in a position where it wasn't necessary to liquidate positions to raise money for redemptions. These managers may be using this weakness as an opportunity to buy shares of stock from no load managers who are forced to liquidate their shares due to redemptions.

As you consider the best manager for you, don't concentrate on the manager's performance during periods when the markets overall did well. Don't clamor into funds which make the cover of magazines. Consider how well a manager performed when the markets were very volatile such as 2000 to 2002. This period in our market's history was one of the most difficult times investor ever endured. Managers who protected investor capital during this period earned every fee they were paid. If the manager you are choosing didn't manage during this period, avoid the fund.

Will a higher fee based manager outperform low fee managers all of the time? Absolutely not. But working with your investment advisor or visiting www.morningstar.com, you will be able to make a decision based upon the managers past performance history.

4.Hire a Manager, Not an Index

In the late '90s and early 2000 several financial and media commentators suggested that mutual fund and high net worth portfolio managers were incapable of outperforming the overall market indices. As the markets moved higher, several mutual funds and managers actually underperformed many indexes such as the S&P 500 and the NASDAQ 100. These commentators recommended investors utilizes a new class of investment called the Exchange Traded Fund (ETF).

Exchange Traded Funds is by definition of pooling of individual stocks that represent specific indices created by research firms. These funds which trade on the New York Stock Exchange and consist of stocks that are part of indices utilized by Wall Street such as the NASDAQ 100 (QQQQ) or the Russell Mid Cap Growth Index (IWM). These funds are not actively managed and will only make changes to the positions when a new company falls out of the index or is eligible for the index. Exchange Traded Funds offer lower fund expenses, little to no management fees, and the ability to buy and sell the fund any time during the trading session, but you get what you pay for.

As an example, many investors decided to ditch their mutual funds in March of 2000 when they realized that their mutual fund manager didn't outperform the S & P 500 Index. Many switched to the Exchange Traded Fund version of the NASDAQ 100 (QQQQ) and the Standard and Poors 500 (SPY). These funds included the same companies which are represented in these two popular indexes. The indexes have historically represented the largest 100 and 500 capitalized companies which trade on the NASDAQ and the New York Stock Exchange. Their thinking was, why pay fees for a manager who can't even beat the markets?

As this book is being written, the Exchange Traded S&P 500 Fund (SPY) is resting at $146 per unit some 38 points BELOW the closing price in March of 2000. Investors who accepted even more risk and purchased the NASDAQ 100 (QQQQ) need to see the index double before they even get back to break even.

Choosing an index over a manager can reduce the fees and expenses you pay each year, but the risk associated with this decision could put you in a position that provides little growth in your assets to combat higher costs in the future.

There are several benefits to hiring a manager, whether it is an individual money manager or a mutual fund manager. In most cases these managers rely upon research attained by their firm to make investments they believe will outperform the markets in the coming years. Their research isn't always right, but over time, many of these funds have shown the propensity to outperform the indices and Exchange Traded Funds

Don't get caught up in the financial magazines and media's portrayal of a managers' performance for a given year. While they may tout his performance as one of the top managers over the past three years, be sure to consider his performance when things were really rocky. It's for this reason that I find a five year track record and the managers' worst performing year the two most important variables I consider when hiring a manager. Usually, a market has time to work through various cycles over a five year period, and if you consider his worst performance year, you can understand exactly the type of carnage that could occur with your portfolio if you selected this manager.

This is not to suggest that Exchange Traded Funds do not have a purpose. They do. ETF's provide many benefits that money managers and mutual funds do not, especially if there is not a qualified fund manager you can select that matches needs you have with regard to your asset allocation plan, but when the markets have a serious setback, it's nice to know that you have a professional who is taking advantage of the weakness to build a portfolio that could help you reach your financial goals for the future.

5. Taxes Should Never Influence an Investment Decision

Allow me to say it again. TAXES SHOULD NEVER INFLUENCE AN INVESTMENT DECISION! During the last major bull market, I had a number of clients who didn't want to sell a position in a particular stock or fund due to the potential tax consequence. It's for this reason that I rely upon the Personal Retirement Road Map to make the decision for me.

Now this is not to say that you shouldn't clean up losses within a portfolio at the end of the year to lower your tax burden, but it is saying that if you buy Cisco Systems for $20 and it goes to $80 in nine months, you should take some of your profit off the table and reallocate the assets according to your recommended asset allocation stance.

As I've mentioned before, there are at least two times you want to review your Personal Retirement Road Map. Historical evidence suggest that one of the best times to review your Personal Retirement Road Map is early May and November. As you review the performance of your equity portfolio and the returns generated over the previous six months, don't wait until January 1 to reallocate your portfolio. I've seen clients wait until the following year to reallocate their portfolio to avoid paying taxes in the current year. By the time January came around, there wasn't a taxable event. Profits had been lost. When you decide not to sell because of impending tax consequences, changes could take place which could eliminate potential gains that could have been profited.

So many investors in the late '90s and early 2000 didn't want to sell their high tech funds or stocks due to the short term capital gains. By waiting until they had a more favorable tax treatment, many of these investors didn't need to worry about capital gains any longer.

6. Taking Inflation for Granted

Think about this ... with a 3 percent inflation rate.... .the value of $100 drops to $76 after 10 years. In 20 years, it's worth $56. While Social Security checks are indexed for inflation, your check may not go as far in your city.

The risk tolerance of retirees is to gravitate towards investments that minimize their risk, but when interest rates are as low as 4 percent the risk of taxes and inflation has them spinning their wheels while the rest of the world keeps moving. Think about it, when was the last time that medical expenses only went up 3 percent in a given year. Do you believe that your company (if your company offers this service) will continue to pay for a large majority of your health coverage as rates continue to move higher?

According to Consumer Price Index statistics from 1985–2004, the average increase in physician services has grown nearly 5 percent annually while prescription drugs have increased by more than 5 percent per year. If you consider that the average retiree is expected to live a minimum of 20 years in retirement, are you able to see how these costs could compound your income situation if you don't protect your income with some growth in your portfolio?

Inflation is one of the main arguments why investors need to accept additional risk in their retirement portfolios and expose all their investment assets to at least 50 percent equity holdings. It's not a necessity that these holdings be in individual stocks. These investments could be mutual funds, ETF's, money managers, or variable annuities which offer guarantees of income and principle. As the statistics point out if you consider taxes and inflation, your purchasing power could have you losing principle faster than you realize.

As an example, consider the chart below. The illustration considers a retired investor who chose to stay conservative and invest a large portion of their retirement assets in liquid assets such as c.d.'s. There's no doubt that c.d.'s can play an effective role in a retiree's investment plan, but to place a large portion of your assets in c.d.'s in order to prevent loss of principle could be more devastating than you realize.

Year	6 Month CD Rate	Taxes	Inflation	Real Return
1996	5.46%	31%	3.32%	.45%
1997	5.72%	31%	1.70%	2.25%
1998	5.44%	28%	1.61%	2.31%
1999	5.39%	28%	2.68%	1.20%
2000	6.63%	28%	3.39%	1.38%
2001	3.53%	27.5%	1.55%	1.01%
2002	1.78%	27%	2.38%	-1.08%
2003	1.19%	25%	1.89%	-1.00%
2004	1.80%	25%	3.25%	-1.90%
2005	3.80%	25%	3.84%	-.99%
2006	4.01%	25%	3.75%	-.74%

* Inflation figures and C.D. rates provided by CDA Wiesenberger 1/07

The example considers the real return on your money if you had invested in c.d.'s which matured semi-annually over the past 10 years and were adjusted for inflation and taxes according to the highest marginal federal income tax rate based on $100,000 of taxable income for a married couple filing jointly (www.Taxpolicycenter.org).

The return on your assets is very important, but it is the real return on your assets that will make the difference in your next 10 years in retirement.

While you may have seen your bank statements rise every year, the ultimate affect of taxes and inflation served as a hidden cancer over the years. In order to fight the affect of inflation and taxes, the only types of investments which have been proven to provide success over time have been those investments which presented risk. If you aren't willing to accept the potential for risk, then you should lower the expectations you have with regard to your income potential over time.

These are considerations you should not take for granted as it relates to your investments. Your Personal Retirement Road Map that is available through www.torrid-tech.com is able to illustrate what the value of your dollar today will be in the future. As you consider allocating your investments for the future, consider these additional factors which could provide you an opportunity to reduce volatility in your investment portfolio and grow your investments in order to meet your future income needs.

11

Can I Do it Alone?

It was June 1, 1937 and Amelia Earhart was embarking on a journey that had never been done by any female pilot, she was about to fly around the world. The journey had her starting in Miami, Florida, and finishing in California. She didn't know exactly how many days it would take her, but she knew the general direction she would fly and would hope to reach her destination in the coming weeks.

The trip was without incident as Amelia and her navigator Fred Noonan had reached the South Pacific. Amelia had no problems successfully navigating her plane during this flight or on other flights such as her Atlantic crossing or cross country flight, as she could rely on land markings to chart her progress, but now that she and Fred were beginning to cross some 7,000 miles of ocean with little to no visible land forms, she would need to rely upon a navigator with experience.

On the morning of July 2, 1937, she and Fred left for Howland Island, their next destination island on their way to Hawaii, but something went wrong. By all accounts it's estimated that she missed the island by some 35 miles. How could things have gone so well for so long? What went wrong? How could they miss an island by 35 miles?

Speculation evolved as to the exact cause of the plane vanishing in the Pacific. Radio transmissions were received from the plane by a Coast Guard cutter ship, but it's evident that Earhart never heard the transmission. Roosevelt had planes and ship search the region for over two weeks and spent over $4 million trying to find the plane or pieces of it, but to no avail.

Experts began to question how Amelia's plane could be so far off course. Many felt it was Amelia and her navigator who didn't have the proper maps and experience needed to cross the Pacific. Some claimed that the jet stream likely pushed the plane off course others suspected the lack of island references played a role. Whatever the reason, at the time of Amelia's last transmission, she was still flying the plane, and the plane was still flying, she simply didn't know where she was.

I tell this story to illustrate just how far you may be able to get into retirement before you need to rely upon the experience of a successful navigator that can help guide you through storms and unforeseen obstacles to help you realize your retirement dreams and goals.

I can't tell you the number of individuals I've seen in my years as an investment advisor, that came to me in their late 50's and early 60's and ask me to help them plan for retirement when they didn't save for the future or work with a professional. These individuals had little to no assets, high credit card debt, and they continued live paycheck to paycheck with no contributions in their 401(K.) Unfortunately, these individuals had waited too long thinking about their retirement, and the answers that I provided weren't the answers they wanted to hear. If I could have seen them 10 years earlier, I might have been able to help.

The primary reason people seek advice is to gather information in order to make rational decisions. Is the advice you receive always correct? No, just as in Amelia's case, the navigator was using a map that was 5 years old at the time and incorrect. Is it possible that you could reach your retirement dreams and goals on your own? Depending on your personal experience, yes but are you willing to fall short of your dreams?

Retirement is one of the biggest journeys of your life and a journey where you should rely upon a financial professional to help you interpret and navigate your Personal Retirement Road Map. People seek advice regarding their taxes, real estate purchases and sells, investments, insurance, and estate planning. Many have the appropriate background where they are capable of completing some of these tasks on their own, but when doubt exists, and questions are raised, that's when you need a professional.

It's scary enough stepping into the world of retirement without the safety net of a steady paycheck. Throw on top of this the fact you now have a nest egg you need to protect in order to get you through your retirement years. There will be times when severe storms will attack your nest and it could likely cause many sleepless nights and raise concerns about your future. It's likely you may have encountered one of these events while you were flying on an airplane. What is it worth to you to have an experienced professional navigate you through these storms?

As you consider choosing a financial professional to help you navigate you through your retirement years, you need to consider someone whom you can trust and who understands the importance of keeping you safe from forces that could negatively impact your retirement. This doesn't necessarily mean that you need to have all your investments with this one person, but he's aware of all the investments you have, so he can monitor your Personal Retirement Road Map and update you on your progress routinely, make adjustments as needed and offer alternative routes in case of storms or detours.

The word professional carries a special meaning for individuals who choose the profession. It's important to remember that many investors assume that because someone works in the field of investments, they have a handle as to what will happen in the markets. This is simply not true. A true financial professional realizes that investing is a long term approach that will have good and bad times. The difference is the professional will insist the client maintain focus on his plan and not how the markets are performing, and make adjustments according to their needs and goals.

Financial professionals are listeners. While they may ask several questions, they want to hear you talk about the issues that concern you and will answer all your questions until they are confident you understand the direction you are taking with regard to your Personal Retirement Road Map. Many will ask questions relating to your needs and goals, take notes, and use this information to derive the proper map for you. They will tell you that the map will change over time, but that when changes need to be made, you will have a thorough understanding as to why the change was made and how it could affect you and your family in the future.

Many investors could avoid trouble and losses if they remember one thing. If you are the one asking a lot of the questions, then you may need to leave the meeting early. A true financial professional will ask questions that are designed to draw out more information from you. They will begin with basic questions about you and your family, and then become more involved with regard to your investment history, needs, and goals.

A professional does not ensure you will generate a specific return each year unless they have evidence in writing or on the confirmation you receive. They will not tell you they can beat the market each year or anticipate every financial concern you may have. They're ultimate goal is to provide you with the safest route on your Personal Retirement Road Map according to your needs, risk tolerance, goals, and timeframe.

A financial professional will provide recommendations and remedies to many of the issues that you face in retirement. If they can resolve them, they will tell you. It doesn't matter if you are a beginner to investing or are considering making a change due to a referral you received from a friend or colleague. It's never too late to start asking questions about the individuals or the firm that will handle your nest egg. It's important to remember it's YOUR money, YOUR dreams, and YOUR livelihood that may be at risk.

How many times do you visit your doctor each year? If everything appears to be in working order, you may only see him a couple of times a year at most, but if you've had health issues that have shown up such as higher cholesterol, high blood pressure, or aching bones, you may seem him much more.

When you meet with your doctor, it's likely his nurse takes your vitals before you actually meet with the doctor. When you meet with him, he's likely pursuing through the notes of your most recent visits and compares the new information he just received. He likely asks you about new medication he may have prescribed and its effects. He's likely to ask you about your sleeping habits, exercise, and any new worries you may be having. In essence, before he provides any type of diagnosis, he's asking a lot of questions about you and your health.

A doctor can only do so much. His education can provide a remedy for ailments he can see as a result of your test, but doctors would like to be as proactive as possible as it relates to your health. If you don't communicate that you've had a pain in your stomach for the past several months that just won't go away, his test may not reflect an issue. This is why it's so important that you communicate with your doctor how you feel, what is concerning to you, and the actions you need to take to sleep better at night.

Communication plays a vital role in everything we do in life, and this will be especially true as you work with your financial professional. While you may have discussions on a monthly basis to update progress or new opportunities, you need to schedule at least two office visits so your professional can review your current financial health in order to avoid potential issues down the road. You may meet with your accountant once (if at all), your attorney (once every five years), or your insurance agent (once every seven years), but you should see your financial professional at least twice a year during retirement.

The meetings you have should discuss where you are with regard to your Personal Retirement Road Map and any potential concerns that need to be addressed such as health concerns, legacy planning, or new dreams you have in mind. These meetings not only allow you the opportunity to review the performance of your account, but it offers an opportunity to fine tune your portfolio and reaffirm your dreams and goals and issues that could affect them in the near future. While some may feel a meeting at the end of the year is appropriate, the best time to have meetings with your financial professional is actually in May and November.

If you think about it this way in late May, your taxes are complete. You have a thorough understanding of what your income was for the previous year and your taxable burden. If you found yourself with more in savings than what you spent, then this information should help you address other dreams and goals you may be considering. On the other hand, if you found things to be a little tight, you may want to consider taking more income from your investment portfolio, or re-evaluating some of the dreams and goals you had in mind.

In November, it allows an opportunity to track your progress before things get out of hand. The holidays will be upon you in no time and if you've discussed gifting with your children, or perhaps taking a nice trip the following year, whatever the reason, it's a perfect opportunity to sit down with your financial professional and see where you stand in your Personal Retirement Road Map.

Another reason that these two months represent good times to meet with your financial professional involves the seasonality associated with the markets. A full chapter *(Chapter 13: Beating the Markets)* is dedicated to the benefits surrounding these periods, but just as you don't let good fruit go bad on the tree, the same should be said regarding your investments. Like every season, there's a time to grow and a time to prune, and these periods provide you with a historical pattern that should benefit your investments for years to come. Do not neglect the importance of this chapter.

Another benefit of working with financial professionals is the information they can provide at your request. While your professional may not be available 24/7, many bank and securities firms offer websites and toll free numbers which allow you visit your investments online 24 hours a day. These firms may also provide the guidance, information, and research you may need to improve your financial decision making and move forward. Your decision making may actually become much easier with the assistance you receive from a financial professional who can integrate all your investment holdings and provide you with a big picture understanding of how your financial decisions impact your Personal Retirement Road Map. Several investment firms today offer their clients the ability to see all their holdings in one place, even though some of the holdings may be held elsewhere. The opportunity to see all your investments in one place not only helps your professional, but provides you with the ability to see how your holdings work together towards your retirement dreams and goals.

Other conditions that may warrant you to seek professional advice could be a sudden change in your life such as retirement, a major illness, the sale of a business, the death of a spouse, or the consideration of a major purchase. All of these are reasons where you may decide to consult with a financial professional who may be able to share insight and advice as to how it could affect your decisions for the future. During these types of events, stress and emotions can run very high, often clouding your personal judgment. There's nothing wrong with seeking the advice and counsel of a professional who doesn't have an interest in your decision, but may be able to provide you with scenarios you can consider before making any decisions.

Financial Professionals Are Not Expensive

Retirees understand that two of their more pressing concerns are health and finances. During retirement, many retirees make every effort to reduce costs to the household. Anywhere they can save a dollar, is a dollar saved towards healthcare costs, prescription drugs, or maintenance issues. One cost that retirees could reduce is their investment costs. There is a perception that financial professionals charge an exorbitant amount of money for their services, whether this is in the form of fees, commissions, or a combination. While some may take advantage of the situation, this can easily be resolved by speaking with a professional and discussing their fees or commissions before you consider working with them. Every person is different as to how they wish to compensate their professional, but before you think about managing your retirement future on your own, remember that all it takes is one incident or mistake, and the dreams and goals you had for yourself during retirement could put you back in the workforce again.

A true professional will outline how he is compensated for his services. In many instances, the investment recommendations he offers will not financially impact. For the guidance and information they provide to you, their fees are inexpensive compared to others who serve in the real estate and accounting world. What's important is you have the confidence that this professional you choose has the ability to navigate you through your retirement.

How Do I Find a Financial Professional that's Right for Me?

You may be in a position where you've never had to rely on a financial professional, but as you get deeper into retirement, many of these professionals have the experience to help you manage your retirement assets. Perhaps your current financial professional lacks your trust and confidence, or you don't anticipate his retirement may come before yours, if this is the case, refer upon other business associates or mentors for a referral of someone that specializes in retirement planning or a firm that offers retirement planning assistance. Be careful when relying on friends and family. Many individuals would like to keep their financial condition private and in case something did go wrong, these relationships could get uncomfortable, especially if you have to see each one another at church or on Thanksgiving.

If you don't have a resource to turn to, you may rely on television, the internet, or other advertising sources for help. Many of the discount brokerage firms today offer similar services as their full service counterparts at a much lower cost to the investor, but the similarities stop there.

I believe a discount firm such as a Fidelity or Charles Schwab can offer outstanding benefits to retirees that can help them plan for retirement, but I believe that's where many of the similarities stop. Their services are good up to a certain point, but at some juncture, you may find yourself in a position where you need a specialist who can navigate the open waters of the Pacific Ocean to insure that you remain safe on your journey, something Fred Noonan didn't offer Amelia Earhart.

If you are comfortable that you understand your dreams and goals and have built a Personal Retirement Road Map to navigate, then by all means I would suggest that a lower fee service firm could help you successfully navigate through retirement, but remember that not only should you be the one expected to navigate your retirement, but you'll also be the pilot as well.

Depending on the firm, many of the investment choices you will need to make will be your responsibility. Some firms may offer their selection of funds or portfolios, but their ability to help you navigate through events in the markets stop there. They're service only goes so far. They listen to you and take your direction, so if you're comfortable talking with yourself, then by all means, these firms serve a purpose.

I can understand the popularity of the discount firm while you are saving for retirement, but when you're in retirement, that's when things really change. You need to rely on a firm, a team, or a person that you know will be there for you to help you along the way. Unfortunately many discount firms simply offer a toll free number you can call, but it's with someone who doesn't have a vested interest in your happiness. They are simply there to answer your questions as it relates to your account.

When conditions in the market make you nervous, it's nice to speak with someone who has a vested interest in your happiness, versus someone who is paid a salary to answer your questions, but not provide advice. Most of us are happy when the markets are going up and are investments are climbing. The difference is consider how you would feel if another 9–11 took place and you didn't have someone to talk with about what impact this event would have on your investments and retirement dreams and goals.

Meeting with a Financial Professional

In your meeting you should never be intimidated or embarrassed to ask any question. A financial professional will welcome your questions no matter how basic they may appear. Experienced financial professionals will encourage you by asking if he is explaining things clearly. These professionals realize that an experienced client is an asset, not a liability. They would rather answer your questions before you commit with them than to confront your anger, anxiety, or confusion later.

When you meet with your financial professional for the first time, you should plan for enough time so that you aren't rushed. In an introductory meeting if the financial professional is recommending a specific investment at that time, you should reconsider if he truly has your best interest at heart. The first meeting should be established as an introduction of the two parties. An experienced financial professional will take the time to ask you serious questions about your investment history, your investment needs and goals, and what you are specifically looking for him to do for you. Remember a meeting with your financial professional should be similar to your meeting with a new doctor for the very first time. The doctor realizes you are looking to create a relationship, but he's not going to tell you what's wrong with you before asking you several questions about your symptoms, your history, and your expectations. Once he runs a few tests and does some research, he will provide some type of remedy for your condition.

The meeting with your financial advisor shouldn't be a one way conversation. You should have a list of questions to ask him. I know if I were visiting a new doctor, I would want to know about his medical background, his interests, how often he's available (late night calls), and who you can see if he's not available. You should prepare these questions and write them down. If you like what you hear and you trust your professional, you may want to have these answers available to you at a future time.

Another benefit of taking notes in front of your financial professional is that it sends a signal to your professional that you are serious and an astute investor. You are showing evidence of trusting the professional but verifying what he is saying is accurate. By taking notes, it tells your financial professional 'words mean something'. An investor who wants to know more about the risks and rewards of investing will continue to document conversations and information provided to them.

Here is a list of questions you could ask when meeting with your financial professional.

First Meeting Questions:

1. What is your experience in providing advice on the topics below?

Retirement planning _____
Investment planning _____
Tax planning _____
Estate planning _____
Insurance planning _____

2. What are your areas of specialization? (You don't want someone who specializes in 401k plans helping you with your retirement needs) What qualifies you in this field?
3. How long have you been offering financial planning advice to clients?

How many clients do you currently have? (This is very important. A good financial planner will not take anyone. They have a specific group of individuals that they work with. Usually referrals come from friend and family members. You don't want someone who has more than 300 relationships. There is simply no way that anyone can administer good service to all these individuals unless it is a team environment)

4. Briefly describe your work history. (There aren't a lot of professionals these days that are new to the business. What is important to know is the history of this professional moving from one firm to another. The more moves, the more concern about his restlessness to stay in a current location or with the current firm)
5. What are your educational qualifications? Give area of study. (A business background is helpful. Don't assume because someone holds a CPA license they are best suited for you. While they may be conservative in their recommendations, they may not have the best communication skills).
6. What financial planning credential(s) do you hold? (CFP is helpful, but not necessary. Be wary of other "credentials" that other professional may tout such as Certified Senior Advisor, Certified Retirement Financial Advisor, or other designation. Many times these designations simply require a check and a week-

end visit for a seminar. Designations aren't nearly as important as the number of years they have been working with retirees).

7. What financial planning continuing education requirements do you fulfill?

8. What licenses do you hold? (This is important in order to verify that a professional is licensed to sell insurance or investments. It provides you with an opportunity to research if any customers have filed complaints against him over the years through one of the available government sites).

9. What services do you and your firm offer to retired investors? Why should I consider your firm? (If you can work with a firm that provides detailed information as it relates to your account, your investment performance, and your personal financial roadmap, these services could be invaluable).

10. Describe your approach to financial planning. (This is a very important question. If your professional insists that his clients utilize a planning tool in order to help them reach their financial goals, it speaks volumes about this professional. If the professional you are speaking with does not inquire about your planning or recommend some form of planning aid, why would you want him to handle your investments? It would be no different than a doctor operating on you without running any tests or taking any x-rays to see what ails you, only accepting your word that your stomach hurts.)

11. Who will work with me on my plan? (Many professionals today have "teams" of members that they work with. This should not be considered a strike against the professional, only to reinforce his organizational skills. These teams have members that perform various tasks from account maintenance, communications, and filing. Questions about account activities such as statements check reorders, and questions on activity within your account will likely be directed to other team members. Make sure you take the time to meet these people so you can put a face with a name, and visa versa. But when it deals with investment decisions and the effect on your personal financial roadmap, verify that the professional you select will be there to answer these questions).

12. How are you paid for your services?

13. What do you typically charge?

All of these are very important questions when you meet with a financial professional

Investment Recommendation Questions:

Is this investment product registered with the SEC and my state securities agency?

Does this investment comply with my risk tolerance and investment needs according to my stated investment goals?

Why is this investment suited for me?

How will I profit from this investment? (Dividends, Interest, Growth)

What are the TOTAL fees including money management fees associated with this investment?

Are there ways to reduce or avoid some of the fees that I will pay?

What is my "net" cost for investing in this recommendation?

How liquid is this investment? If I needed money from it, partial or full amount, what would be the cost to liquidate? How long would it take to get my money back?

What is the risk with this investment? What is the maximum I could lose? How does this relate to my risk tolerance for loss?

What economic or domestic factors could change the risk of this investment? (I.e. higher interest rates, tax law changes, recessions)

Where can I get more information on this investment?

What Type of Professional is Right for Me?

Finding the right financial professional to help you during your retirement journey will be a very important step towards reaching your dreams. These professionals can be found at brokerage firms, banks, insurance firms, or accounting offices. Many of these professionals have been educated thoroughly with regards to the markets, financial planning, and tax issues. Many continue their education by receiving advance certifications such as a CFP (Certified Financial Planner), CLU (Chartered Life Underwriter), CPA (Certified Public Accountant), or a CSA (Certified Senior Advisor). These types of credentials have historically reflected continued education where they have specialized in a particular type of financial planning that can help clients plan for the future, managing their insurance, assisting with their taxes, or working primarily with retirees and senior issues.

While everyone should have a doctor who serves as their general practitioner, would you trust him to do open heart surgery? Of course not while he may have gone to medical school, he hasn't had the practice. This is why it's important to hire professionals to manage your financial affairs who have experience and practice in such areas. Your general practitioner should serve as your liaison between specialists you may need in your life. Your general practitioner provides a game plan for you to maintain good health, but when conditions arise and a specialist is needed, he's there to provide you with the best person to help you.

An experience financial professional should be able to refer you to specialists in all areas that will affect you in retirement from tax issues, to insurance issues, to estate issues, to investment issues. What is important is that you find someone who understands the issues you will be encountering in retirement and works with you to create and monitor a map that is designed to help you meet the needs and goals during retirement. When a specialist is needed, he will be there to refer him to you.

Most retirees will find themselves in need of an attorney, an accountant, an insurance professional, and an investment professional. Depending on your expertise, you may feel as though you could substitute some of these positions and save some money by doing it yourself, but remember, the markets, insurance laws, estate laws, and tax laws change on nearly a annual basis. If you're going to do this on your own, you must make the commitment to educate yourself and continue to educate yourself as conditions change. If one of these is considered your financial professional, it should normally be an investment professional, simply because of the potential day to day contact you may have with him regarding financial decisions and the impact on your Personal Financial Road Map.

How do I pay for services?

Cost is a large component that affects many seniors today. Every dollar saved may one day be needed in the future, but the cost of "saving" money may ultimately "cost" you money in the future.

Financial professionals charge for their services in many ways. Before you decide to work with anyone, make sure you understand completely how they are compensated. Regardless of the investment you make, someone is being compensated for it. You may not see it, but the cost is there.

Some of the various ways that professionals are paid include:

- A commission
- An hourly fee
- An hourly fee plus commission
- A fixed fee or a retainer fee
- A fee based upon the value of the assets
- Some combination of the above

Depending on how you choose to pay for these services is up to you. Most professionals will be willing to work with you in order to make sure you are comfortable with the amount, but make sure you fully understand how the professional is being paid and the ultimate effect it could have on your investments.

It's important to understand that while you may consider doing your own taxes, or making your own mutual fund investments with no load firms, the greatest cost may come when you actually have made a mistake and your portfolio can't recover. The information and research available on the web today is overwhelming and in many cases confusing. The dollars you invest in working with a financial professional may avert potential problems down the road by doing it yourself.

Many retirees try to manage their financial future much like their visits to their doctor. When they're sick, that's when they make the visit to the doctor. If they feel everything is fine, they don't see the reason to make the investment. All it takes is one of those days when you don't feel well to change everything. The purpose of preventive medicine is to catch potential problems before they become larger issues. Regular visits to your doctor and financial professional is part of a preventive routine.

The more time you spend with your financial professional the more time he can help you interpret and navigate your Personal Retirement Road Map and overt costly mistakes. You shouldn't allow cost to be the main determinant as to whether you work with a financial professional. When you're sick cost is no object. When it comes to reaching your dreams and goals during retirement the cost of securing these dreams shouldn't be either

Big or Small?

As you begin your search, there will company names you may or may not recognize. Some professionals may work with larger firms that are experienced in the investment marketplace and their firms offer resources such as portfolio performance, monthly statements, insurance protection of your assets, and financial roadmaps that provide detailed information as it relates to your assets.

Some professionals may choose the road of being self-employed and not affiliated with a major company. This freedom allows them to recommend several investment opportunities that may not be offered by the larger financial institutions. While you may gain the ability to step into their office for individual attention, the research, support, and resources may not be available.

Another important consideration to make in dealing with a professional is the protection of your assets. Typically the larger financial firms will monitor the portfolios for their clients and verify that the risk tolerance and investment objectives are in accordance with the clients' wishes. In many cases their oversight provides the opportunity for you to receive information from a third party that could influence your investment decision. These larger firms understand the importance of making sure the investments match the needs, goals, and risk tolerance of the client. Not for the protection of the firm, but for the protection of the client.

As you deal with smaller self employed financial professionals, it's important to understand that this resource may not be available to you. Depending on the type of investment vehicles you choose, your investments may or not be protected by insurance that is offered at the larger firms. While many of these smaller firms offer an outstanding service to their clients, the last thing you would want to see as you prepare to meet with your professional is an office that's been vacated.

Check Their Credentials

If you would like further information on the financial professional that you may be considering to help you manage your investments during retirement, here are some independent sites which provide information as it relates to their experience and any past issues they may have had with other clients:

CPA   State Board of Accountancy
Financial Advisor   The National Association of Securities Dealers www.nasd.com or 1-800-289-9999
Registered Investment Advisor   www.sec.com or 1-800-732-0330
Insurance Agents   State Insurance Commissioner
Estate Planner or Tax Lawyer American Bar Association

All of these sites will provide you with a history of the professional you have chosen including any actions, complaints, or restrictions on the professional.

Some other areas you may want to consider as mentioned by the NASD website include:

- Ask the professional about

  - Areas of specialization
  - Professional designations
  - Registrations or licenses
  - Education
  - Work history
  - Investment experience
  - Products and services
  - Disciplinary history

- Understand how you will pay them for their services. Investment professionals are typically paid in one (or more than one) of the following ways:

  - An hourly fee
  - A flat fee
  - A commission on the investment products they sell you
  - A percentage of the value of the assets they manage for you
  - A combination of fees and commissions

- Ask whether they receive any additional compensation or financial incentives based on the products they sell. Sometimes investments professionals and their firms receive additional compensation for selling a particular mutual fund or other investment product.

- Make sure that the investment professionals and their firms are properly registered with NASD, the U.S. Securities and Exchange Commission or a state insurance or securities regulator and learn about their professional background, business practices, and disciplinary history. Most investment professionals need to register as investment advisers, investment adviser representatives or brokers (registered representatives). Others may only be licensed to sell insurance the NASD website (www.nasd.com) can help you find registration and other background information on these professionals.

- Check out any professional designation by contacting the issuing organization and determining whether they are currently authorized to use the designation and whether they've been disciplined. Make sure you understand the requirements for a professional designation. The criteria used by organizations that grant professional designations for investment professionals vary greatly. Some require formal certification procedures including examinations and continuing professional education credits. Others may merely signify that membership dues have been paid. You may also use the NASD website to find the appropriate website or telephone numbers for a specific professional designation.

- If the investment professional will sell you investment products, ask if the firm they work for is a member of the Securities Investor Protection Corporation (SIPC). SIPC provides limited customer protection if a firm becomes insolvent. Ask if the firm has other insurance that provides coverage beyond the SIPC limit. SIPC does not insure against losses attributable to a decline in the market value of your securities. Learn more about SIPC protection at www.nasd.com.

The role of the financial professional is to navigate you through your retirement future as a work in progress that has a map which offers various routes to potential goals. Sometimes detours will be necessary due to market conditions, your personal circumstances, or changes within the investment selections, but ultimately he will provide you with the information and recommendations to get you back on the path towards your retirement. To assume that your financial professional will be able to foresee every potential roadblock, obstacle, or event along the way is unrealistic. His job is to provide you with the best facts and information at the time, and provide a solution that represents the best course of action to help you get back on track.

The financial professional wants you to succeed in reaching your retirement dreams and goals. He serves as your navigator who is not only there to interpret the markets, but to listen to you and provide solutions for you. No one wants to see you reach your dreams and goals more than he does. He gains personal satisfaction in knowing that his efforts have helped you reach your dreams, protect your wealth, and provide for your family. So when you consider whether you really need the help of a financial professional, ask yourself this question, do you really want to navigate through retirement alone?

12

Stay Organized

Remember those nights when it was your turn to be Santa and your son or daughter wanted that special toy that needed to be put together on Christmas Eve? How many times did you get it right? Inevitably there's always some part that never made it into toy, thus something didn't close right, spin right, or look right. If you had just followed the instructions and taken the time to get organized before Santa's arrival, it likely could have meant a chance for you to get to bed a lot earlier.

While you may look forward to retirement, the process itself has several parts which when fitted together can make retirement a truly enjoyable journey, but like a toy that has a few pages missing from its manual, there's a lot to deal with.

During your retirement you will need to deal with Social Security, Medicare, retirement income, managing your nest egg, insurance issues, parents, children, grandchildren, and a whole host of other things. Its likely most of these issues will impact you at some point during you retirement years so if you can prepare yourself in advance and take steps to be organized during retirement, it could enhance your quality of life.

Between junk mail, catalogs, and flyers it's easy to feel overwhelmed when it comes to paper. Even papers that are important such as bills and statements seem to pile up in a corner somewhere until you find a few minutes to review them. There's more that you want to do with your retirement life than sit down and pay bills, but it's a necessity that you will have to face. The sooner you take steps to get organized in retirement, the sooner you can be off towards doing the things you've dreamed of doing.

Getting organized may seem like a daunting task at first, but it is absolutely essential. Think about how much less stressful Christmas Eve would have gone if you had taken the time to put the toy together a few nights before, rather than telling Susie that Santa left you a note to go to the hardware store to get a missing bolt that an elf misplaced. If you had taken the time to get organized, you could have had the proper tools, and if something was missing, you could have had the opportunity to return the toy or find out where you may have made a mistake.

Organization during retirement covers several aspects. Organization involves everything from your daily activities, to your financial affairs, to your long term dreams and goals. Think about it this way, when we are organized, we have a plan or routine in place. We usually have an idea as to what we are going to do, when we will do it, and how long it will take. When we understand the process, we gain confidence in our actions.

Part of organization is managing your budget. In the first chapter of this book we discussed that before you start spending in retirement, you needed to know your expenses. Too many retirees find themselves unprepared for retirement. They never took the time to understand where they were spending money and now they bring a heavy debt load into retirement. If you have no idea how much money you are spending, then take the next three months and record every expense you have and balance this against your income.

This doesn't mean you need to buy a computer or software program, paper, pencils, and notebooks work extremely well. You need to see where money is coming in and where money is going out. If you find that after taking care of important bills such as utilities, mortgages, credit cards, insurance, and household expenses there is still money remaining, you're better off than most, but if you find yourself in a position where your inflow isn't covering your outflow expenses, please take the time and review *Chapter 6: Finding More Income*.

You may find yourself where you've encountered expenses which are part of the budget such as paying off a home equity loan, credit cards, or college expenses. It's fine to have these expenses in the budget as long as you don't find yourself going into debt. What is important are the good habits you create as you follow and review your budget. This process will avoid potential detours in the future.

If you're computer savvy an excellent source to help you track your financial matters such as income, spending, and investment information is Quicken or Microsoft Money. These programs and many other financial software programs offer the ability to input the information from many of the documents that come into your house. They also offer you the ability to see your household budget online and make payments to merchants, utility companies, and other companies that you make regular payments to.

The Quicken and Microsoft software will work with your bank and provide up to date information as it relates to financial matters for the household. Some companies allow you to download information from your investments so you are able to see a snapshot of where you are on your Personal Retirement Road Map. Remember Torrid Technologies provides a recommended version of the Personal Retirement Road Map. A subscription to their service is provided for you by visiting www.torrid-tech.com.

If you're not computer savvy, don't worry about this. Not everyone is comfortable with them and it's perfectly acceptable to use a loose leaf notebook that has dividers, sections, and paper in them along with file folders that can fit into a fireproof storage box. How you keep track with your budget is up to your own personal taste, but if you have the time, I would recommend taking a computer class to get comfortable with computers. Several companies which sell computers offer classes at their store and the software programs that are available to retiree could mean you spend more time outside doing the things you enjoy versus inside reconciling a balance sheet.

Another suggestion that can help you stay organized is to pick a day of the week that you review information you've received in the mail or things you need to address. This time should be a time that you set aside to place bank, brokerage, or other statements into the folder, writing checks, or reviewing past charges. If you've written checks, record your records and review your budget to verify that things are very close to your actual budgeted expenses. Minor fluctuations are fine, but you need to be aware of significant increases in costs as they could eventually eat into your personal income. Every time you have an opportunity to review your budget provides you with an opportunity to gain confidence in the steps you are taking are helping you reach your retirement dreams and goals.

Most utility companies and other bill providers can change your billing period to reflect one that is comfortable with you. I usually advise people to have their bills come during the same period in the month so that all their important information such as bills or expense occurs at one time. When bills and information come during various times, it's easy to misplace something. When you know bills are coming, you know what to look for.

You should consider allowing utility companies, mortgage companies, and credit card companies to draft your payments directly from your checking or savings account on a monthly basis. These are companies you will depend on in the future and you do not need to skip or miss payments to these companies. If these expenses are drafted from your checking account every month, you won't need to worry about having your utilities shut off for lack of payment.

As I mentioned before Quicken and Money are two great software programs which can assist you in the budgeting process during retirement, but banks and brokerage firms have also made great strides to provide budgeting software capabilities to their clients as well, so if you have a relationship with your bank, ask them about what their company can do to help you budget your household during retirement before you invest in another program that may not be necessary.

Somewhere in your computer it is good to have a contact list of key individuals in your life that are helping you in some form or fashion in retirement. This list could include your banker, lawyer, financial consultant, preacher, life insurance agent, children, and others. You should also find a place that records account numbers with various financial institutions you may rely upon as well as where key documents are kept such as a safety deposit box, safe, or fire proof box.

One of the problem areas that we see as a nation is that too many couples don't share information with the other. In many cases it's the wife who is unaware where her husband kept files, important documents, or accounts. Make it a habit that your spouse is very clear about where this information is kept. There are thousands of cases where the government and financial institutions take control of assets that should have gone to family members. If you are the sole surviving spouse, make sure someone in your family is aware of the assets you own and where they are located.

Something else you should know about computers and that is sometimes things do go wrong. If you are utilizing a computer to budget your household and you have important information stored on the computer, make it a habit once a month to save your data, and at least once a year, copy your data to another saving device that is not connected with your computer. Keep a hard copy somewhere other than your house and in your computer such as with a child or in a lock box. If something happens, this information will make it easy for you to pick up where you left of in case your information is lost.

If you choose to stay away from computers, you need to consider creating a notebook that holds your key financial information. There are key sections you need to have along with some valuable information.

Your notebook should contain the following sections:
Personal Retirement Road Map
Personal
Accounts
Investments
Insurance
Taxes
Estate
Correspondence
Other

Let's break these down one by one.

The most important section should be your Personal Retirement Road Map or Plan that has been prepared for you by a financial advisor or yourself. This document serves as a source to help you reach your retirement needs, goals, and dreams. It's important that you take the time to review this as you sit down to complete your bill paying process each month. Take the time to review the reasons you saved for retirement. What was the purpose of building the nest egg? How are these funds being utilized? Are my items being budgeted properly or am I spending too much or not enough? Is the amount of income coming into the household enough to maintain the household? How are my investments performing relative to the goals and expectations set? Are there adjustments that need to be made?

The Personal section should include key information about you such as social security numbers, key contacts you have such as the executor of your wills, your attorney, insurance representative, your financial advisor, your minister, your best friend. This section is designed so that if something happened to you or your spouse, information would be available to help you find what you're looking for, or at least give you contact information of someone who may know.

The Accounts section will list all your accounts including profit sharing plans, pension plans, deferred compensation plans, savings, checking, credit cards, loan accounts, and any other "account" where you have a relationship. This would make it easy for a loved one to understand all areas where you may have a financial relationship.

The Investment tab is simply used for investments that you may have with brokerage firms, banks (c.d.'s, savings bonds, money market accounts), annuities, 401(k) plans, mutual fund companies, limited partnerships, and personal trusts.

The Insurance tab should hold copies of policies that you have. DO NOT HOLD ORIGINAL POLICIES IN THIS NOTEBOOK. Original policies should be in a safe place such as a fireproof box, safe, or a bank deposit box. This section should list specific information on not only the type of policies you may have such as life, long term care, disability, flood, auto, home, umbrella, but also the agent of record, contact information for the company, the policy number, when the annual or semiannual premiums are due, the policy owners, beneficiaries, and where the policy is located.

The Tax tab should contain your tax reporting document for the prior year including all schedules sent to the Internal Revenue Service. In many cases your tax attorney or accountant will have a record of tax returns filed over the past three years which is the legal right for the Internal Revenue Service to audit your returns after you have filed them.

The Estate tab should have information about your wills, living wills, trust documents, and power of attorneys including executor for your estate. You may not feel comfortable having copies in your notebook, but you could provide information as to the name of the attorney who drafted these documents for you and where originals are kept.

The Correspondence tab is information that comes in from time to time directed to you about a specific subject. It may not fit with a specific tab, but it's noteworthy enough for you to keep.

The Other tab is for the remainder of information you find interesting and want to review for another time such as mutual fund reports, interesting articles from newspaper or magazines, or newsletters.

There may be other tabs you may want to add such as Real Estate which would include information about other properties, business or lease agreements you have with others. Consider all other areas that are important to you and include them in your notebook.

Once this information is complete, share this information with a trusted advisor so he retains a copy, and perhaps provide a copy to one of your children who may be the executor of your estate. Should something happen to you, these individuals could have access to information which could be vital to your well being. If you're not completely comfortable providing this information or making it public, consider having a copy in a lock box in the house or at the bank where one of your decedents is able to access it.

These are just a few steps you that will go a long way towards helping you stay organized during retirement. They will not only provide you with information when you need it, but they will serve as a constant reminder as to where you are in the retirement process and the progress you are making towards your dreams and goals.

13

Beating the Markets

As you're driving down the interstate, how many times did you notice a lottery billboard that had a huge jackpot and thought, "I would love to win that"? Can you recall times when you made a bet on a low priced stock you hoped to double overnight? Or maybe it's hitting a jackpot in Vegas.

Most of us can only hope that an opportunity would come our way, but while I can't provide you with the next winning numbers for the upcoming lottery or inside information on the next company that's about to be bought out, I will share with you information that is not widely known, but could make a dramatic difference in the performance of your investments now and during retirement.

Over the years there has been much debate as to whether it is truly possible to time the markets. Timing refers to one's ability to buy and sell at the appropriate times prior to a change in the markets' or stocks' direction. Most brokerage firms, mutual fund companies, and money managers will simply state it's not possible. Their research suggests a long term investment plan is the best course of action for serious investors, yet day traders and stock promoters will sell you on their abilities to successfully trade the markets everyday.

So who's right? Is it possible to time the markets?

In my opinion, YES but not in the traditional sense.

There's a phrase that I believe will always remain true and that is, history tends to repeat itself. I've seen many examples in my life of this saying, some good, some bad, but what you are about to read in the remaining portion of this chapter should provide the confidence you need to act at the right time and produce returns which could significantly outperform other investors who have never believed historical trends. Whether you choose to accept these statistics as truth is up to you, but remember this, numbers never lie.

Everyone should be familiar with the term snowbird. This term has been used for years to define retirees who have homes in the chilly north as well as a retreat in Florida. These bi-residents will routinely pack up their home up north around late October, and begin their trek to their winter respite in Florida where the weather is not as harsh. In late April, early May, they reverse the trend and begin the drive back north where they avoid the harsh summers of Florida and enjoy the cooler summer nights in the north. This makes perfect sense if you can afford it. It's an opportunity to have an ideal climate 365 days a year. What these snowbirds may not realize, is that the markets operate in a similar fashion.

Seasonality

Since the 1950's the stock market has operated in a predictable seasonable pattern similar to those of snowbirds. What many investors have not realized is if these patterns had been followed, they would have had an opportunity to see their investments outperform during a favorable market trend and protected when the trend was not so favorable.

From a weather perspective, I can certainly understand why someone from upstate New York would choose to migrate south around the beginning of November. I can even understand why they are looking to head back north around the first of May. These two periods offer ideal climates in opposite ends of the country, but what I can't explain or will try to rationalize is why the markets produce higher returns from November through May, and why the markets perform poorly during the period of May through November by more than a 7–1 margin.

Did I Just Say 7 to 1?

Since 1950, Stock Traders Almanac (www.stocktradersalmanac.com) has kept a statistical summary of the performance of the Dow Jones Industrial Average during two six month time periods. The first investment period begins May 1 and ends October 31. The second period begins November 1 and ends April 30. The almanac illustrates that risk is worth the reward November through May.

This historical trend may have been the reason the phrase "Go Away in May" was coined on Wall Street. Whatever the reason for this phenomenon, and many experts have their opinion, this is one of the primary reasons I recommend retirees review their Personal Retirement Road Map every May and November. It certainly makes practical sense for a number of reasons such as after tax season and before the holidays begin, but the more important reason is to make adjustments to your investment portfolio where you can take advantage of the seasonal trends the markets provide.

In order to provide a better example of this advantage of what this might mean to you and your investments in the future, let me tell you a story about a couple of brothers who proved this theory to be correct.

Larry and Darrel Stenson were brothers living in Iowa in 1949. These brothers had worked for nearly 15 years on their large family farm when their father realized that neither of the brothers had an interest in keeping the farm in the family. The father decided to sell the property and give Larry and Darrell their share of inheritance early.

Larry and Darrel were your typical brothers who remained competitive while they were growing up. They rarely agreed on anything so when it came time for them to decide on the best way to invest their money, each one agreed to invest their money in the Dow Jones Industrial Average. But Larry wasn't happy that Darrel had already invested his money. He found out that Darrel took his $100,000 and invested it on May 1. Larry decided to sit on his inheritance for a while until he could wait no longer. He contacted an investment house and invested his inheritance in the stock market on November 1 of that same year. Darrell heard of Larry's investment and immediately sold his positions. He held his money until he could wait no longer, so on May 1 of the following year, he entered the market once again. Larry then repeated the pattern, pulled his money out, and thus the pattern continued this way for more than 55 years, each brother pulling their funds out, Larry on May 1 of every year and Darrel on November 1 of every year.

Fifty seven years later Darrel, who chose to put his money in the markets on May 1 and take it out every November 1, has decided to use some of his money to help his grandchildren with college. Upon contacting his advisor, he has seen his $100,000 grow to $103,310 after 57 years.

Larry, on the other hand, who decided to take his money and invest it every November 1, and withdraw it every May 1, is planning on paying the full tuition for his grandchildren, buy them a new car for college, and buy land for them to build their first home as he has seen his $100,000 grow to $5,340,000!

The average compounded return on Darrel's money, not considering inflationary damage, is. 06% while Larry's compounded annual return is 7.55%.

You may be asking yourself if these trends will continue. It's in our nature to question. If it works so well, why doesn't everyone follow it? The simple truth of the matter is that all of us are different. The times we choose to buy and sell depend on our needs or emotions at the time.

In my years within the financial services industry, one of the toughest decisions that an investor makes is the decision to sell. When their investments are doing well, they want to get the most from their investment (GREED), and when their investment is doing poorly, they are afraid of seeing the nest egg damaged any more (FEAR), but those investors who rely on their Personal Retirement Road Map and meet with their financial professionals every May and November, have no problems making these decisions.

If the historical trend for the markets suggests that the period of November through May represents the best opportunity for the markets to perform, this would mean that when you review your Personal Retirement Road Map in May, the exposure you have to investments which are geared towards growth such as stocks, may reflect a higher percentage ownership than what your Road Map suggests, therefore you would sell some of your equity holdings, and reinvest these assets in the areas of your investment allocation which are deficient, which have historically represented investments which offer income and historically have provided less risk.

Conversely, as November approaches and you review your Road Map prior to the holidays beginning, the markets may have fallen over the summer and thus your fixed income holdings may have performed well, and your equity holdings may not have performed very well, thus you would sell some of your fixed income holdings, and reinvest those assets into the equity markets.

It's much easier to sell stocks and buy c.d.'s than it is to sell c.d.'s and buy stocks. Stocks are risky and c.d.'s are safe. In the beginning as you trust this seasonal pattern, your emotions will likely interfere with your decision making process. They will likely remind you that you're selling assets in May that have performed well, and you're selling assets in November, which make you feel comfortable due to market volatility. This is why you need to rely on your Personal Retirement Road Map and the recommended investment allocation for your investment portfolio. By following this seasonal pattern, you not only have the opportunity to see your investments outperform the markets over time but you have the opportunity to build confidence in the years to come and take advantage of opportunities when events occur.

Could there be a time when this strategy doesn't work? Absolutely, but since 1950 no one has determined a better time period for investors to review their portfolio. By taking the time to review your Personal Retirement Road Map during these periods, you have the opportunity to review the performance of your holdings, sell positions that need to be paired back, and protect your nest egg during volatile periods.

Bullish Percent

It is said that the United States economy trades in cycles. About every four years our economy has seen an economic slowdown followed by a recession, a recovery, and then expansion. During these periods the stock markets can fall as earnings from corporate America fall short of expectations. In some cases these periods create a period where the market volatility is very high as investors choose to sell their stock positions and transfer to the safety of guaranteed investments.

The imbalance that takes place within the markets can create an opportunity for investors. There is a technical indicator which provides statistical and historical information you can use and gives you confidence to reallocate assets from your safer holdings such as c.d.'s, money markets, and bonds, and invest them into the stock market. This indicator is called the Bullish Percentage Index.

The Bullish Percentage Index is a mathematical calculation derived from a form of technical analysis that tracks the percentage of stocks which are trading in a "bullish" or upward pattern versus a "bearish" or downward pattern relative to their point and figure analysis. Now this may seem like a pretty intense definition, but it's really easy to understand because the Bullish Percentage Index actually paints a picture that is clear and concise.

Point and figure analysis was created in the early 1900's when Charles Dow began recording the closing prices of stocks each day. He began to gather more and more information until he noticed that the stock prices over time provided a pattern. These patterns were diagramed by an "X" for an advancing issue and an "O" when the issue declined. Over time he began to see technical and statistical analysis which pointed to trends as to whether the demand to own a stock was greater than the supply available. If there was more demand, he would be able to see the stock forming more "X" patterns as the stock continued to move higher in price due to more buyers in the system.

In 1955, a company named Chartcraft (now known as Investor's Intelligence) used Charles Dow's point and figure charting technique to develop a broader market indicator which incorporated stocks that traded on the New York Stock Exchange to determine the direction of the market as a whole. Each evening after the close of the market the Bullish Percentage Index is calculated by identifying the number of stocks which are flashing a bullish or buy signal relative to the charting rules of point and figure analysis. This percentage is plotted as its own chart after every closing day which has a vertical and horizontal axis ranging from 0 to 100 and a time value from one year to the next. What is important is not to let the definition overwhelm you, but let the graph paint a picture for you as to whether you should be aggressive or conservative when it comes to investing in the markets. (see chart example Appendix A near back of book)

An intriguing aspect about this type of analysis is that everyone can understand it and find it. You don't have to figure the calculations on your own. The Bullish Percentage Index is calculated for you for stocks which are represented on the New York Stock Exchange, the S & P 500, the Dow Jones, the NASDAQ, and a host of other indexes. The information can be found by visiting www.stockcharts.com and typing in the search page for the index you have an interest in. I prefer to use the New York Stock Exchange index simply because it covers the largest majority of stocks that trade in the markets.

The Bullish Percentage Index isn't a fast moving indicator. It is an intermediate index which is perfect for most long term investors. It is designed to show you the flow of money, whether it's flowing in or out of stocks.

Historical evidence points out that there are times when the Bullish Percentage Index reaches levels of extreme and pessimism. It's during these times when you should become cautious and bullish, which coincidently usually operate just the opposite as you may be feeling. Allow me to explain.

When the New York Stock Exchange Bullish Percentage reaches a level of 70 percent, it signifies that 70 percent of the stocks which trade on the New York Stock Exchange (more than 6,000) are in a "bullish" pattern as it relates to their point and figure analysis. In essence, 70 percent of the stocks in the market are moving higher. As you and I both know, the markets are due for corrections or set backs from time to time.

For some reason the Bullish Percentage Index has always been an early warning signal for investors which provides an opportunity to protect their investments at a time when they may be feeling good about what they own. In August 2001 prior to 9–11, the Bullish Percentage Index flashed a SELL signal when it reached a high level and reversed lower. Can you imagine how different you would have felt on 9–11 if you knew you had taken the necessary steps to protect the equity portion of your nest egg?

There are times when the Bullish Percentage Index reaches extreme levels of pessimism. This occurs when the index falls to a level around 30 percent or lower. This suggests that according to point and figure analysis, 70 percent of the stocks trading on the New York Stock Exchange are in a down pattern and the markets may be ready for a reversal. When the Bullish Percentage Index reaches this level, this is a time for you to become extremely aggressive as it relates to your stock portfolio. It should serve as an early warning signal to GROW your investments at a time when you are scared about risking your nest egg in the stock market.

The Bullish Percentage Index is it is a mathematical formula and offers a historical track record. If you question its success I encourage you to review its past history. The Bullish Percentage Index is based upon statistics without the interference of human emotion or analysis that could skew the results. This makes it a pure mathematical formula which has been tested over time and because we haven't seen our emotional base change over time, it provides a great resource you can use to see how the markets reacted during other volatile times in our nations history so that you have the confidence to make the right investment decision based upon fact, not emotion.

On September 22, 2001, the Bullish Percentage Index flashed a buy signal when it reached an extremely low level of under thirty percent. There are very few times in history when these conditions exist, but could you imagine the conversation you would have had with your investment advisor at that time? We had just been attacked by terrorists and there was continued conversation of more attacks and war. It's likely you may have been selling equity positions in your nest egg when you should have been buying!

When the Bullish Percent Index reversed from such a low level, the S&P 500 index was near 1000. By December the S&P 500 had reached 1150, a gain of nearly 12 percent in a couple of months!

This would serve as an example of how Bullish Percentage Index can help you manage your investments during periods of high stress or uncertainty. Even if you had not taken advantage reallocating some of your safer assets in the market at the time, this index should have given you the confidence to at the very least hold your equity holdings and surrender to the emotions of others.

Unfortunately too many investors rely on the media for their news and information. Over the years I've consistently told my clients that some of the best investment opportunities are when no one wants to watch CNBC or get a call from their broker. Some examples of these times would have been right after the crash of 1987, 9–11, October 2002, and March 2003. All of these periods represented a time when an *event* took place and affected the markets for the short term. When scary periods such as these occur many investors go into protection mode. Rather than looking at the potential opportunities they concentrate on protecting their nest egg when most of the damage is already done.

There have been other times when the markets did very well such as 1991 (end of the Gulf War), 1996 (internet in its infancy), and January 2000 (Y2K was a non event). Retirees tuned their televisions to the financial channels in the late '90s. They clamored for new companies coming public for the first time and tech stocks that weren't forecasted to make a penny for years to come, and as the bottom fell out, did they sell? Unfortunately no, many of them bought more shares, but why?

It's so important during volatile times in the markets you rely upon your Personal Retirement Road Map and your financial professional. There will be times when you will take profits and protect capital, but your decision should be based upon statistics and historical evidence which gives you the opportunity to maximize your investment returns and grow your nest egg.

By following the seasonality that the market provides as well as relying on the statistical evidence that the Bullish Percentage Index provide, you may be able to increase the returns from your investment portfolios over time and secure your nest egg with stronger branches to withstand any potential storm.

14

Buy a Ladder for Income

I can remember as a young adult looking forward to my birthday. It wasn't that I was looking forward to a party or birthday cake, it was the opportunity to open up mail and collect my checks!

If there is something all investors have in common it's the thrill of going to the mailbox and receiving dividend or interest checks from stocks, bonds, or c.d.'s. Retirees especially look forward to these days since the income that comes in provides them with a sense of security that their investments are paying off.

If retirees could invest their nest egg in guaranteed tax free income and never have to worry about money the rest of their lives, then this would be a sound strategy, but as we know, unfortunately most retirees could be faced with investing as much as 50 percent of their nest eggs into the stock market, which means the selection of assets that will provide you with stable principle and interest over the next 20—plus years needs to be invested in a fashion that provides you with the highest interest return possible with the least risk exposure.

If you follow the recommended strategy of allocating 50 percent of your investments within the equity markets, it may be prudent to consider allocating the remaining assets in investments which not only offer income, but stability of principle. Each person's needs are different. Some investors are able to invest in c.d.'s, while others need to consider investments with a higher degree of risk. What's important is to understand the how the risk is different between the two.

It's no different if you have two paths you could take to a destination. One path will get you there quicker, but it requires driving on untested roads. The other path is a smooth interstate that will take longer, but why expose your vehicle, or assets in this case, to uncertainty if you know another path will get you to your final destination?

As we learned from a previous chapter, your asset allocation may recommend as much as 50 percent of your assets be invested in income producing investments that offer a fixed rate of return on a monthly, quarterly, or semi-annual basis. These income producing assets are not only an additional source of income to the household during retirement, but they have historically provided stability during volatile times in the markets, but there are two elements of risk that can affect them which are credit and interest rate risk.

Credit risk is the risk you take in owning an asset that is a pledge by a company, bank, or government. When you purchase a c.d., the bank is providing you a rate of return for using your money. The credit risk to this investment is low as many c.d.'s are insured by the Federal Deposit Insurance Corporation for up to $100,000. But there are other investments whereby a company may borrow your money, but depending on what happens to their business, may never return these funds again. This is the risk you take based upon the credit of the issuing company.

Another form of risk that can affect you in retirement is interest rate risk. Interest rate risk occurs when you make an investment for a specified period of time and interest rates move higher over time, thus the return you are receiving on your money isn't as high as it could have been if you had not invested at a longer term.

In the '80s many retirees remember interest rates at 15 percent, but yet no one had an interest in buying long term c.d.'s or government bonds in fear of seeing rates move higher. Investors who chose not to lock in these long rates missed out on an opportunity of a lifetime.

I've learned in my twenty years watching the markets that it's nearly impossible to predict the direction of interest rates. What I have found in my experience is when you think rates are as high as they can go, they will always go a little higher, and when you think that they can't go any lower, they usually find a way to go lower. The best practice I've found is as you allocate assets into fixed income investments such as c.d.'s, and bonds, reduce credit and interest rate risk by building a strong ladder.

There's always been a misconception when it comes to buying c.d.'s. Most investors believe if they invest more money with the bank they could earn a higher rate of return on a c.d. While it's possible you may receive a little bit more than the advertised rate, the interest rate risk you take for investing more dollars into that one c.d. could cause a detour on your Personal Retirement Road Map.

It's true that c.d.'s, treasury bonds, and other insured investments which provide income offer guarantees, but the guarantee is only the return of principle. Many investors fall into the trap of jumping on the highest return they can earn on their money for a period of time, or they invest in the shortest maturity in fear they may need the funds. These types of decision could cause just as much damage to an investment portfolio than a 10 percent correction within the stock markets.

Think back to 2002 when interest rates were low and the markets were in freefall. Emotions overtook stock investors as many reallocated their nest egg out of the stock market and poured it into c.d.'s and short term guaranteed bonds. To these investors it made sense. We were in a recession getting ready to go to war. These were very tumultuous times.

As more and more investors began pouring money into c.d.'s and government bonds, and the Federal Reserve continued to lower interest rates to spur economic growth, interest rates fell to levels below one percent. Many investors not happy with these rates chose to purchase c.d.'s and bonds offering rates as low as 3 percent for five years. They weren't concerned about what their rate of return would be as long as the principle would get returned. As long as they continued to hold onto the investment, their principle would be returned, but what did they lose over that five year period of time?

The markets rallied from 2002 through 2007; inflation rose by more than 3 percent and banks which had offered less than 2 percent for one year c.d.'s, were now offering nearly 6 percent. In essence, these guaranteed investments actually caused many retirees to reconsider their dreams and goals as the markets passed them by. If they had just considered laddering their fixed income investments, they could have not only been in prime position to take advantage of the market weakness, but their fixed income assets would have been locked in at higher rates.

The concept of *laddering* a fixed income portfolio is very simple to understand. It represents exactly what you think, a ladder. A ladder has steps that lead up to a higher rung. The rungs are spread out in a fashion usually about a foot apart in order to help you reach where you're going without a lot of separation in between the rungs.

Now imagine a ladder that had the rungs spread out two feet apart. While you can still get to your destination, it may not be the safest or the easiest way to proceed. If the rungs get spread out even wider, it's nearly impossible to reach where you need to go.

Laddering your portfolio simply means dividing the total amount of your nest egg that should be allocated in fixed income over equal periods of time.

As I mentioned before, the best people on Wall Street can't tell you where interest rates are headed. They can predict, prognosticate, and analyze, but the bottom line, it's still a guess. Unlike the equity markets which have shown a propensity to continue to grow over time, the interest rate market does not beat in lock step with the equity markets. They are impacted by market events, world events, and governmental decisions. They can be very volatile or tame for a short or long period of time. In essence, the interest rate market beats to its own music and none of us can hear it.

Because of this no one can predict where interest rates are headed. Any one occurrence could change the course for a long period of time. We may be able to predict in the short term (six months or less) the direction of rates, but for periods longer than a year, it's nearly impossible.

It's my opinion that banks aren't interested in talking with you about a laddering strategy. Their concern is simply to get your money so they can loan it out to others at a much higher rate. It doesn't matter to them if you invest in a six month, one year, or 10 year c.d. All they want is your money.

When you rely upon the banks to help you find investments which offer income, it's easy for them to offer you a little more interest. They realize it's a hassle for you to get in your car and drive down to the location. That's why today they send a notice in the mail to you that tells you, 'if we don't hear from you in the next seven days, we will automatically roll your c.d. over for another year, usually less than your previous rate. How many times do you actually get these notices where they roll the c.d. for a higher rate? Yet retirees continue to trust banks.

I understand that with 50 percent of your assets invested in the stock markets, it's important the remaining portion of your nest egg stay safe, but this doesn't mean it can't work for you. If you decided to invest all your fixed income investments into a 6 month c.d. or a U.S. government bond fund, based upon what you've heard or believed, could devastate your nest egg. It would be no different than investing all your money in Wal-Mart stock because you read in a magazine they were expanding into China. You are gambling.

Remember, no one can predict the direction of interest rates, so if we have no idea where interest rates are going, and a large portion of the nest egg needs to be invested in investments that offer income, how do we do this?

Let's assume we have two retirees who come into the same bank branch to buy an advertised one-year c.d. offered at four percent. They each had a total of $50,000 to invest. The first retiree spoke with the bank representative and told him that he would invest the entire $50,000 in the one-year c.d. if he could raise the rate. The branch manager told the investor that he would offer an 18 month c.d. at 4 ¼%. The investor felt like he won and took the deal.

The second retiree took a look at all the rates available at the bank. He saw the following rates:
1 year 4% 2 year 4.25% 3 year 4.5% 4 year 4.75% 5 year 5%

Based upon this information, he decided to split his $50,000 up equally amongst these five maturities. By doing so, he would earn an effective yield of four and a half percent on his money the first year. After one year he would need to reinvest the $10,000 that came due from the first year c.d., but he would simply roll the proceeds into a new five year c.d.

After eighteen months, the first investor came back to the bank to renew his c.d. He had received a notice from the bank that they could renew the c.d. for 3 ½ percent for one year. The investor rolled his c.d. over for six months at 3 percent, feeling confident that rates would be moving higher next time.

After six months had passed the first investor came back to the bank and was offered 3 percent for one year or 3 ½ percent for 3 years. Unhappy with his previous decision, and not wanting to see a lower rate, he rolled the c.d. for 3 years at 3 ½ percent.

The second investor continued to purchase five year c.d.'s as each c.d. matured. Over the next four years, he purchased five year c.d.'s that paid the following interest; 4.75%, 4.50%, 4.25%, 4.0%.

After five years had passed, the first investor who placed all his $50,000 investment in a c.d. for an eighteen month, six month, and a three year c.d. received total interest of $8,437.50 The second investor who laddered his $50,000 over a five year period received total interest of $11,250 over the same period.

Are there circumstances when the first investor would do better over time? Perhaps, but in order to reduce volatility, provide access to principle, and provide for consistent income, a laddered portfolio offers the highest rate of consistent income return which does not adversely income your income needs each year.

Investors who gamble on trying to lock their money in on the highest rate of return for the shortest period of time could get caught in a very difficult trap where they have depended on the income from a high paying investment over the years. Now as the investment matures, the options available to them offer substantially less income. This type of action could create additional amount of stress as they try to find a suitable replacement, consider cutbacks in their life, or perhaps live on some of the principle.

By laddering the portfolio any changes within the interest rate market should not materially affect your standard of living of the expected annual income you should receive from your fixed investments.

Occasionally you may find yourself in a situation when you need to replace a car. What better place to draw assets from than a fixed income investment that is about to mature. You may have other investments available where you could draw from, but they may have tax consequences. As fixed income investments mature, it allows you many options as to whether to reinvest the proceeds, use them to replenish your savings or checking accounts, or use them for an upcoming expense. You may find yourself in a position where your other investments are in a position where you do not want to draw down from them, and having fixed income investments that mature often could provide you with added capital at when you need it most.

Many c.d.'s have penalties if you should break the contract with the bank. In some cases this could result in a loss of interest and principle. If your fixed income portfolio or c.d.'s were laddered, the loss of principle on a $10,000 investment would be more manageable than having to break a $50,000 certificate of deposit.

In this chapter we used the illustration of certificates of deposit as an example, but this type of strategy works with all types of fixed income investments including annuities. A qualified advisor will be able to assist you in identifying the investments that are appropriate for you based upon your risk tolerance, tax bracket, and income needs. What will be important is to determine just how tall your ladder will be.

15

Annuities in Retirement

Mention the word *annuity* and you're likely to various responses such as 'never heard of them', 'what do they do?', 'won't ever do that again' to 'best investment I ever made!' If anything, a conversation about annuities can generate reactions similar to a good or bad restaurant experience.

Too many times annuities are recommended to investors for the features and benefits they provide. Guaranteed income, principle protection and the ability to defer taxes are enticing attributes with any investment product, but with these attributes come a price. It's up to you to determine whether the investment into an annuity is worth the price.

An annuity is an investment contract which is offered through an insurance company. The annuity contract is similar to life insurance contracts. If you have owned life insurance contracts in the past, especially whole life or variable life contracts, then the structure of an annuity should be familiar to you.

There are primarily three key individuals associated with the annuity; there is an owner, an annuitant and a beneficiary. The owner of the annuity contract has the ability to withdraw funds from the annuity contract at any time prior to the death of the annuitant. The annuitant is the insured life which could be the owner or another person. In many cases, the annuitant is usually the spouse. Upon the death of the annuitant, the beneficiaries are entitled to the proceeds of the annuity. The annuitant is not entitled to any funds during any time and while you may change who owns the contract or who should benefit from the contract at any time during the life of the annuitant, the annuitant cannot change.

Annuities are a contract. There are provisions within the contract which will explain the role, responsibility, and commitment of the insurance company. The contract will contain important information as to who is the owner of the annuity (the person who could liquidate the annuity, make changes to the investments, take withdrawals, etc), the annuitant (the person's life on whom the contract is insured upon), and the beneficiaries (the recipient of the annuity upon the death of the annuitant). The annuity contract also contains information concerning early redemption penalties or surrender charges, riders, and maintenance costs, just like a life insurance contract.

There are primarily two types of annuities. A *fixed* annuity, in which an insurance company will offer a guaranteed rate of return for a specific period of time, and a *variable* annuity which offers several "sub accounts" inside the annuity which allow the investor to invest the assets of the annuity into funds which are managed by some of the top portfolio and mutual fund managers today.

Annuities are similar to Individual Retirement Accounts in that they permit you to invest and delay payment of taxes on your investment earnings until you begin withdrawing funds. Because they are designed for retirement, they carry the same penalty of an Individual Retirement Account, in that if you withdraw funds from the annuity, prior to age 59 ½, without reasons allowable under Internal Revenue code, then the funds you withdrawal would not only be subject to income taxes, but also a 10 percent early withdrawal penalty.

Annuities are popular and more appropriate for investors who are age 50 and older who need to invest more funds towards retirement without having to worry about capital gain or income tax issues. By the time someone reaches age 50, they are usually in the peak income earning period in their life. Their children are nearing graduation from college and disposable income begins to grow again. Utilizing annuities could defer additional income inside investment accounts which defer income taxes and gains until another period of time.

Several concerns arise when conversation turns towards an investment in an annuity. One of the more frequent and just concerns surrounds the issue of surrender penalties or early withdrawal penalties. Just as a c.d. may have a penalty for early withdrawal, there are some annuities which carry similar penalties which could invade your earnings and principle investment.

Most annuities have a declining surrender charge penalty schedule. This means that if you decide to cancel your contract in the first year or break the provisions of the contract, a penalty could be charged on the amount which exceeded the allowable limit for redemption. Details regarding penalties associated with your annuity should be discussed with you prior to you making an investment by the agent soliciting the contract to you. If this did not occur, these penalties should be outlined in the contract you receive from the annuity company. These penalties usually dictate how many years you must retain your assets with the insurance company before they are lifted. In some cases there are no penalties, with some companies, the penalties could be as long as twelve years. If your agent has not taken the time to discuss potential penalties with you in advance of making your investment, do not use this agent.

The scamming of retirees and seniors has become a sore spot with many state regulators and senior watch groups. Many states now require agents to provide the investor with the surrender charge schedule in writing before they invest. This has changed the way that many insurance companies now present their product. Many companies today offer the opportunity for you to invest in their annuity with no surrender penalties for early withdrawal. These types of contracts could not only offer you the tax deferral you are looking for towards retirement, but the opportunity to withdraw funds at any time.

Annuities have evolved over the years so much that now several companies offer annuities with zero surrender penalties or sales charges, even after the first month. These types of annuities are the most advantageous to investors simply because you receive all the benefits which annuities provide without the worry of surrender charges if your contract is broken. There are literally thousands of contracts that are available to investors and an independent broker or insurance agent should be able to provide you with a full list of companies that meet your needs.

Now that we have a general idea as to how annuities work and some of the benefits and pitfalls, let's get down to more specifics as to whether annuities should play a part in your investment portfolio.

Why Should I Consider an Annuity?

When it comes right down to it, there are some really good reasons retirees should consider annuities. Over the years as the industry has changed, investors have forced many insurance companies to enhance the features and benefits of the annuities offered to their investors.

Many insurance companies have added several enhancements, management options, and guarantees which make annuities more attractive than ever before. Unfortunately due to past histories there may have been some investors who had a bad experience or read about the pitfalls of annuities and have never considered them as an option, but believe it or not, annuities could be the best investment you will ever own.

Immediate Income—Insurance companies of today offer various types of annuities which will guarantee the specific return for the remainder of your life or the life of your spouse. These annuities are called immediate annuities because they begin to pay immediately. Immediate annuities are, in effect, private pensions. The annuitant (investor) invests money with an insurance company, which agrees to pay a fixed amount back to the annuitant for a period of time. Typically, the insurer agrees to make monthly payments for the duration of the annuitant's life with a guaranteed number of years of payment, known as a "term certain." For instance, an annuity for life with a ten-year term certain would pay out every month as long as the annuitant lives. If the annuitant dies within the guarantee period, it would pay out for the duration of the 10 years to whomever the annuitant names as beneficiary.

The income tax on immediate annuities is generally lower since a large portion of the income received is principle being returned to you. Immediate annuities provide a guaranteed stream of income that is not affected by the vagaries of the market. It saves the annuitant from worrying about how to invest his or her savings and whether or not the nest egg will last a lifetime. Annuities of this sort should only be purchased from the most financially sound insurance companies so that there's as little risk as possible that the payments won't be made. The biggest problem with relying on immediate annuities as a principal source of retirement income is that they typically are not adjusted for inflation. What may be an adequate monthly income stream today may not be in 10 or 20 years.

Inflation Protection—You can customize annuities to ensure that your monthly paycheck will keep pace with the cost of living. This is critically important because inflation can have a devastating effect on your assets. The downside of an add-on like inflation protection is that it will cost more—in an initial cost or in lower starting payments to begin with.

Principal Protection—One of the best features of fixed and variable annuities is that the value of the annuity can be guaranteed to be at or above the amount invested. You can guarantee that you (or your heirs) will receive back at least as much money as you invested in the annuity and as the annuity continues to grow; your guarantee is locked in every year to a higher level.

Tax Efficiency—The purchase of an annuity allows you to defer income or capital gains from your investment until you need the income. Compounding interest in a tax deferred account can add up quickly over time. Annuities are one of the few investment vehicles in which you have control as to when you pay your income taxes on capital gains, dividends, and income.

Portfolio Protection—Investors who own stocks or mutual funds may not make investment changes in their accounts due to potential tax consequences. Many variable annuity companies today allow investors to liquidate funds within the account without any 1099 being issued. As long as the proceeds remain inside the account, it will not generate a taxable event, so if the funds within your account have grown, you have the ability to take profits without incurring taxes.

Perhaps the best features of the annuity today are the opportunity to protect income from your retirement assets for life.

Opportunity for Lifetime Income—annuities could provide you with the opportunity to earn an income stream whereby you or your family is guaranteed periodic payments for as long as you live or for a certain period of time. The only risk of you living a long and happy life is borne by the ability of the insurance company to continue to make payments. As long as the insurance company is around and doesn't fall into receivership with the State, your beneficiaries will be guaranteed income for the remainder of their lives.

An earlier chapter recommended that for a 65 year old retiree to guarantee his income for the rest of his life, they should consider placing 50 percent of his assets in the markets. As scary as that may sound to you right now, consider the story of Bob and Nora Campton and how an annuity not only saved their retirement, but possibly saved their marriage.

Bob Campton was a saver. During their marriage Bob and Nora lived within their means saving for a home, college, and retirement. After working 35 years for a local corporation, Bob was ready for retirement at age 64. He had planned on retiring in 2000, but the markets downturn had him convinced to stay a little longer in order to rebuild some of his assets in his 401(k), but then came 9–11.

Bob became very concerned about his retirement future so he converted his investments including his $500,000 401(k) and moved everything to a money market account as soon as the markets opened for trading later in the month. He knew things would be different, so he decided to jump while the jumping was good and announced his last day with his company would be December 18, 2001.

Bob was expected to receive a nice pension from his company and with Social Security, he and Nora would be able to live comfortably, but they wouldn't be able to travel as much or help their children. The stock market damage of 2000–2001 knocked the wind out of Bob's 401(k). His balance had fallen more than 25 percent from its peak in 2000, and they weren't in any position to lose any more. Their focus shifted to protecting their nest egg from further damage; that was until a conversation they with a friend convinced them otherwise.

Bob ran into one of his friends who congratulated Bob on his recent announcement. As the conversation turned to what he and Nora would be doing in retirement, Bob enlightened his friend about the damage that took place within his retirement funds. The friend recommended an advisor he worked with and trusted. The advisor was local and Bob knew that while he could leave his 401(k) at his work, he would like to have more investment options so he and Nora could grow their assets and do the things they've dreamed of. Bob contacted the advisor and arranged for a meeting.

When Bob and the advisor met, the advisor was empathetic to Bob's concerns. The advisor listened to Bob talk about all the plans he and Nora had for their retirement future, but the past couple of years in the stock market had them readjusting their thinking. Bob discussed how he would like to withdraw 5 percent from his retirement every year so he and Nora could travel and spend time helping the kids. The advisor assured Bob that he would be able to proceed with these plans as the performance of the fund mangers over the past several years would not only allow Bob to withdraw these funds, but he would likely see the account continue to grow.

The conversation sounded very good to Bob. The information shared by the advisor convinced Bob that he shouldn't be scared of the market because of a couple of bad years. He understood that the markets have periods of underperformance. This was an opportunity for him to work with a trusted advisor who had done very well for other clients in the community. He discussed his plans with Nora and agreed to sign the paperwork to move his assets from his 401(k) account into an IRA.

Bob moved his $500,000 401(k) account into his IRA on December 30, 2001. The advisor and Bob had discussed several mutual fund managers to invest with. Most of these managers were growth oriented managers. The markets were continuing to move higher and Bob didn't want to miss out on the opportunities the New Year would present, so he followed the advisor's recommendation and looked forward to retirement, or so he thought.

By spring 2002, Bob became concerned about the lack of movement in the IRA. He had been collecting monthly checks for $2,250 each month, but his retirement account continued to fall below his original investment. By summer Bob noticed that his funds had dropped significantly lower than his original investment at the beginning of the year. He had a semi-annual check with his advisor, and the advisor assured him this was a temporary block and should be used as a buying opportunity. During that meeting they agreed to transfer more of his assets into the more aggressive funds in order to take advantage of the markets weakness.

As fall approached and Bob received his September statement, he began to panic. The value of his retirement account had fallen to $307,000. He couldn't sleep anymore, he was losing weight, and his relationship with Nora was very tense. She never bothered him about the finances, but as she began to question what he had done, the relationship of forty three years suddenly began to take a turn for the worse.

Bob finally couldn't take it anymore. He made an appointment to meet with his advisor to discuss a course of action. The previous action placed Bob in a position where he had seen years of hard work lost. He simply reached a threshold where he couldn't stand anymore losses to his retirement. He instructed the advisor to sell all the mutual funds immediately and buy a 5-year c.d. yielding 3 percent.

By the time this transaction was complete, Bob's IRA was valued at $321,300. He would receive income of $9,639 per year for the next five years as he waited for his c.d.'s to mature. The dreams he had for himself and Nora were gone. He cried Uncle, and the markets had won.

Unfortunately there are thousands of couples like Bob and Nora who experienced this exact situation in 2002. What is unfortunate is how Bob's advisor never considered the idea of protecting retirement assets through the use of annuities, if he had, Bob and Nora lives could have ended more like the following story.

Allow me to introduce you to the real Bob and Nora Crampton. Everything you know about Bob and Nora up to the point that Bob met with the advisor is true with the exception that Bob's advisor recommended one minor change, that Bob should secure his retirement assets by investing them in an annuity.

The annuity offered Bob several guarantees such as a guaranteed income stream that could only go up over time, a minimum death benefit payable to his wife in the event of Bob's death, and the opportunity to lock in his principle value and guaranteed minimum income each contract anniversary date.

Bob still needed income each month from his retirement account so he and Nora could travel and help their children. They agreed to withdrawal the minimum guaranteed monthly amount from their annuity, which was a monthly payment of $2,291 for the remainder of Bob's life. On December 31, 2001, Bob made the investment and began taking distributions in January 2002.

Just like the spring, he was concerned about the retirement account not keeping up with the amount of income being pulled from the account. In the summer, he met with his advisor and discussed how the value of the retirement account had continued to drop. They reallocated the portfolio and decided to move into more aggressive funds.

When Bob received his September statement, he was sick to see how the value of the annuity had dropped to just over $300,000. He contacted his advisor and was quickly reminded that regardless of the current value of his annuity today, he was still guaranteed to receive $2,291 every month for the remainder of his life. This idea actually provided Bob with a different mindset. It gave him the opportunity to wait things out in order to see just exactly if the market could recover. In essence, he had enough time to not allow his emotions to get the best of him. As 2002 came to a close Bob's and Nora's patience paid off as the value of the annuity regained some of its lost value and had climbed back to nearly $384,000. Bob was glad he didn't panic in October.

Bob and Nora were comfortable letting the annuity complete its mission of providing income for life with an opportunity for growth. The monthly check they were receiving was very comforting to them. They haven't had to change their lifestyle during retirement and have enough time to allow their assets to grow. While their nest egg may have cracked, they are still able to live in their nest and do the things they always dreamed about. The guarantee of income or return of principle allows them the opportunity for the market to come back and by having this guarantee.

By 2007 their time in the annuity had paid off. The markets had recovered and Bob and Nora enjoyed a new stepped up monthly benefit from their annuity. In 2006 they began receiving guaranteed monthly checks for nearly $2,400 each month and the total value of Bob's retirement account had climbed to nearly $550,000.

So while some experts and financial articles encourage you not to consider using annuities, especially variable annuities, as an investment option for your Individual Retirement Accounts or other retirement assets due to high fees and expenses, hopefully Bob and Nora's situation will shed some light on the positives annuities can provide during retirement.

What are the Downsides of Annuities?

Every investment you make in your life will have an element of risk associated with it. It doesn't matter what the investment may be. A c.d. has risk, a money market account has risk, and we all know stocks have risk. What is important is that you are aware of the risk and you make the decision to invest once you understand the potential risk.

Annuities are an investment and they have risks as well, so let's take the time to review some of the risks associated with annuities that you need to be aware of.

Not All Annuities Are Created Equal—The world of annuities is an evolving place. While many annuity companies offer many of the same features and benefits, it's important to read all the information detailed within the prospectus before your purchase your investment.

For the most part there are two basic annuities, *fixed* and *variable*. The fixed annuity offers a guaranteed rate of return for a specified period of time. This rate is determined and guaranteed by the insurance company. This type of annuity is best used for individuals who are concerned about volatility and are looking for a defined rate of return, but there are downsides. The rate and your original investment are guaranteed by the insurance company. There have been times when insurance companies have fallen on hard times and have created a risk.

In the early '90s, several large insurance companies were taken over (or received) by the state in which they were located. These companies had not invested their assets wisely, and had broken covenants enforced by the state. These companies fell into receivership, whereby the state insurance commissioner seized the assets of the insurance company. Today, states are more stringent in order to prevent these occurrences from happening again, but if it were to occur, you may find yourself with no access to your assets or income for a definite period of time. Unlike c.d.'s, fixed annuities are not guaranteed by any government organization, but these annuities offer a valuable benefit to investors who are looking for consistent income over a period of time and are looking to defer income tax as long as possible.

The variable annuity has become a more popular option for annuity investors over the years. The variable annuity offers the same tax deferral features of income and capital gains, but it also allows the investor to invest in mutual funds without having to worry about immediate tax consequences. These annuities allow investors to invest in the markets without worrying about capital gain or income taxes until the owner decides to withdrawal the funds. Over the years, these annuities have become even more attractive as insurance companies now offer investors the opportunity to have their investment guaranteed or guaranteed to grow a certain percentage.

These guarantees are offered by the insurance companies are paid for by you through a rider in your contract, and the insurance company will guarantee your income and principle amount, but unlike the fixed annuity contract where the assets are held and managed by the insurance company, the variable annuity assets are actually held by the mutual fund managers, the insurance company is only the bookkeeper, insuring that no taxes are charged. This is not something to be concerned about and it is a good thing. If your insurance company were to fall into receivership, then these assets would be returned to you because they were not being held by the insurance company, but rather by the mutual fund manager. So while the insurance company may no longer be able to guarantee your minimum income or principle, at least you would receive your current asset value in return.

Internal Fees of Annuities—Regardless of the investment or the relationship, all of us hate paying fees, but we understand it's a necessity in life and annuities are no different.

In return for the tax deferred growth, professional money management, reporting practices, retirement income certainty and preservation of your investment provided by fixed annuities, equity indexed annuities, or variable annuities, you forgo the opportunity to make bigger returns by investing your money in assets that fluctuate in value outside of the annuity shelter.

Fixed annuities offer a guaranteed return over a period of time, similar to a c.d. The fees associated with these annuities are many times built in the percentage rate guaranteed. Equity Index annuities and variable annuities offer the opportunity to invest funds within the market, but have higher M&E charges (mortality and expenses). These are the charges the insurance companies charge for the tax deferred features and other reporting services provided by the insurance company. In many cases, these charges will include guaranteed death benefits that guarantee the original value or stepped up value, whichever is greatest. Mortality and expense charges can eat away at the overall returns of your portfolio as these fees are taken out on a daily basis, similar to the fees that are charged by mutual fund managers. The insurance company withdraws these fees on a daily basis along with the fees charged by the fund managers. These fees could lower the potential return of your investment over time. What you need to decide is if the added expense is worth the tax defer status and the guarantees offered by the insurance company.

Penalties—As we discussed earlier, annuities can be less flexible than other retirement options. Depending on the insurance carrier, an annuity contract may penalize you for an early withdrawal if you need to access your principle prior to the ending of the surrender charge schedule displayed in the contract. Usually the first few pages of your contract will display the penalty for withdrawing a percentage of your principle investment. One of the primary reasons for these penalties is so that the insurance company can recoup some of the commission they paid the agent who sold you the policy. If your contract does not have a surrender fee schedule, then you don't need to worry about surrender penalties, but other penalties may affect some of the feature of your contract.

Another penalty to be aware of is the penalty that is charged by the Internal Revenue Service for early withdrawal. The IRS doesn't care if the investment you made in the annuity is a "qualified" or "non-qualified" account. A qualified account is money that has never been taxed such as a retirement account, a 401(k), or a 403(b). A non qualified account would be money that you've already paid taxes on, and you've reallocated funds from a savings account into an annuity.

If you are under the age of 59 ½ and you choose to make a withdrawal from an annuity, even if there is no surrender penalty that is charged by the annuity company, and you're receiving income from the annuity on a monthly basis, the IRS will receive a 1099R from the annuity company which informs them of the distribution and the IRS will levy a 10 percent tax for the years in which you received the distributions.

Annuities were originally designed to serve as a secondary retirement source for individuals who were looking to put more money aside for retirement without having to worry about tax liabilities. To assure this, the government has levied a penalty for those individuals who withdrawal funds from their annuities.

There are circumstances where you are allowed a distribution under the law that would not be subject to penalty by the IRS or the insurance company. Most of these relate to health concerns such as the need to cover nursing home care, but before you consider making the purchase it's important that you consider all the potential penalties that may be associated with the contract before you make the commitment to buy.

Annuities Misnomers: in Medicaid Planning

In recent years, immediate annuities have become important tools in ensuring the financial health of spouses of nursing home residents, but unfortunately too many investors have been misinformed with regard to what is and what is not allowable under Medicaid laws.

An immediate annuity is an annuity that provides an income payout that cannot be broken until the death of the annuitant or the end of a term. This is a contract that cannot be broken and many agents have recommended these annuities as a way to disqualify assets from Medicaid laws. To have annuities disqualify as an asset under Medicaid laws, the annuity must be immediate. This means that payments must begin immediately. It must be actuarially sound based on life expectancy tables published through Medicaid. This means that the guaranteed pay-out cannot exceed the average life span at the current age of the annuitant when the payments begin. The life expectancy table for Medicaid is not the same as IRS tables. The payments must be substantially equal. Some agents suggest that you could accept lower payments over the term so that a "balloon" payment is made to the family upon your death. According to Medicaid laws, there cannot be a balloon payment at the end of the pay out period or death, whichever occurs first.

Once the annuity is purchased it must be irrevocable, and it can not be assignable. This means you can not sell it back to the insurance company for a lump sum, and you will be unable to sell it to a third party in return for pledging the pay out to the third party purchaser prior to the annuitant's death. In essence, once you decide to invest assets in an immediate annuity, wheels are in motion to pay you income for the rest of your life. There's no turning back. This could cause serious trouble should a spouse or loved one find themselves in a position where they need a large amount of assets immediately. Before you consider "locking up" these funds, make sure that you have enough assets to cover unexpected events that may occur in your life.

Another point you want to consider is the health of the individual whose life the annuity is being written against. While Medicaid does not hold families responsible for unforeseen events or generally poor health, there are occurrences when the proposed annuitant has been determined to be terminally ill, with a limited amount of time of expected survival. In this event, a guaranteed term that is in accordance with the Medicaid life expectancy tables could be considered a "gift" to a secondary beneficiary if the annuity is transferred to another beneficiary, and Medicaid could request reimbursement and penalties from the benefactor.

Annuities as Charitable Gifts

Many retirees would like to leave behind a gift to a church, organization or some other charitable cause, but they would like to consider receiving income from their gift. A charitable gift annuity (CGA) allows you to make a gift to a charity and receive not only a sizeable tax deduction but also fixed annual payments, a portion of which will be tax free as well.

A charitable gift annuity enables you to transfer cash or marketable securities to a charitable organization or foundation in exchange for an income tax deduction and the organization's promise to make fixed annual payments to you (and to a second beneficiary, if you choose) for life.

A variety of resources—cash, stocks, or bonds—can be used to establish a charitable gift annuity. The donor of a charitable gift annuity receives an income tax deduction in the year of the gift equal to the difference between the amount paid to the charity and the value of the annuity reserved to the donor. A fixed portion of each annuity payment is tax free, calculated based on the age of the annuitant. When appreciated property is given, the donor pays capital gains tax on only part of the appreciation. If the donor is also the annuitant, the capital gains tax is spread out over many years.

Annuity payments can begin immediately or can be deferred to some future date, allowing donors to enjoy the charitable income deduction immediately and receive a guaranteed income later—for example when they retire and are in a lower tax bracket. By contrast, a child who is providing financial support for a parent may want to establish an immediate charitable gift annuity for the parent.

The child would receive an income-tax deduction and the parent would receive income for life.

The older the annuitants are at the time of the gift, the greater the fixed income the charitable organization will pay. The Committee on Charitable Gift Annuities sets annuity rates for all charities to follow. Although it is not mandatory that the rates be used, most charities that offer gift annuities voluntarily adhere to the rates.

Example: Mrs. Generous age 82, gives $100,000 to Favorite Charity in return for a single life annuity. She will receive an annual annuity payment of $9,400. Her charitable income tax deduction will be $46,922.90 the year the gift is given, or spread over five years following. Of the $9,400 received each year, Mrs. Donor can exclude $6,394.80 as tax—exempt income for ten years. The gift is excludable from estate taxes. (Calculation is for illustration purposes only; for your actual benefits, consult your attorney or financial advisor.)

While the regulation of charitable gift annuities varies from state to state, almost all states that regulate charitable gift annuities require the maintenance of financial reserves, annual filings with the attorney general of the state, and compliance with other regulatory requirements.

Keep in mind that all bonuses are really just a gimmick to increase sales. A bonus has to be made up somewhere during the life of the contract. This often leads to product designs which will make up the bonus through lower interest rates in future years.

Are Annuities Right for Me?

Unfortunately with all the various opinions about annuities in the world today, there is not a clear cut answer as to whether an annuity serves the best interest of a retiree. There are many variables to consider such as past history, education and understanding, and your personal needs. There are several reasons as to why you should or should not consider annuities as part of your personal investments.

Take the time to consult with your financial professional as to how annuities could play a part in your Personal Retirement Road Map. Several of the factors you should consider include your need for growth, dependable income, time horizon, risk tolerance, tax deferral, and estate planning. While these investments may contain unpopular drawbacks, more popular investment choices offer drawbacks that could be just as devastating to your plan. The main question you need to ask yourself is this, is it worth the peace of mind in knowing your principle and income is protected for life should something happen in the markets that could devastate the goals and dreams you have for you and your family during retirement. If so, annuities should be a part of your Road Map.

For more information about annuities, take the time to visit various website discussions that provide both the pros and cons on annuities.

http://www.pueblo.gsa.gov/cic_text/money/annuity/annuities.htm

www.hartfordinvestors.com

In summary, an annuity is a great way to protect your quality of life in retirement. Your retirement assets can be efficiently used to purchase guaranteed income to last as long as you need. Best of all, this income can be protected from inflation and other financial woes.

16

Retirement Plan and IRA Distribution Issues

According to the 2007 survey provided by Employee Benefit Research Institute, the percentage of Baby Boomers that have set aside or are setting aside funds towards retirement remains very high. This is very good news considering that these future retirees may rely on these assets during retirement, but many fail to take action to ensure their family benefits from years of savings.

Life is unpredictable and there could be situations where you or your spouse may not have the opportunity to enjoy or need the savings from your retirement accounts, but this doesn't mean the government should benefit from your years of savings. As you create your Personal Retirement Road Map, it's a perfect opportunity to review the rules and regulations which cover retirement plans and IRA's.

Current law mandates that when you reach the age of 70 ½, you must begin taking distributions from your retirement accounts. Failure to do so could result in large penalties which could negatively impact your nest egg. In most cases, the custodian who retains these assets for you will make you aware of mandatory distributions, but what happens if you never have an opportunity to benefit from these assets. What happens if your life ends before you have an opportunity to enjoy the fruit of your hard work?

Retirement accounts make up a large portion of many retirees assets. It's important that you understand your rights so that your family and heirs have the opportunity to benefit from your years of hard work. Here are key points you need to consider that could affect your retirement assets in the future:

1. Name a Beneficiary

In my experience I have witnessed many families fall into a situation where a loved one has died, and the retirement account or IRA has passed on to the spouse. This is rational in the scheme of things, but problems occur when the spouse who inherited the IRA didn't name a new beneficiary for the IRA. Upon the spouse's death, if a new beneficiary is not named, the estate becomes the beneficiary. This creates the potential for estate and income taxes, which could result in nearly 50 percent of the total value of the account going to the government in the form of taxes and penalties.

To illustrate: Assume a 45 year old daughter recently settled her mother's estate. The mother maintained an IRA with a value more than $50,000. The mother had not begun taking distributions from her IRA. If the daughter, who is the sole beneficiary of her mother's IRA, chooses to take a full distribution from her mother's IRA, she could risk a significant increase in her income tax, which could result in net proceeds of only $25,200 just enough to buy a new car or pay for college tuition for a year or two.

Now assume that the mother had named her daughter as the beneficiary of her IRA and decided to take advantage of IRS laws to *stretch* her required withdrawals over the next 38.8 years, which is what the IRS says the daughter's life expectancy will be, and the IRA grows at an annualized rate of 8 percent per year. Over the next 38 years she would withdraw $303,113 before the IRA would be depleted. This could result in her being able to buy a new car every 3.2 years!

A large majority of the assets you will collect during your lifetime will come from your house and your retirement account. While the value of your house is estimated in your estate, your retirement assets could suffer catastrophic damage if you have not established a beneficiary who is able to benefit from these proceeds in the future.

There is no restriction as to the number of beneficiaries you can name as it relates to your annuities, IRA's, or retirement accounts. You could name your children, grandchildren, or other individuals or charities as a benefactor these assets. In some cases, as illustrated in the previous example, current tax laws could allow your beneficiaries to grow the proceeds and help them in the future with their retirement planning or other needs. Verify your retirement accounts have named beneficiaries who you would like to benefit from your passing. While your will could name the benefactors to your IRA if no one is named, the current tax laws available to you today could ensure that a large majority of the retirement assets you saved for the future, go to your family instead of the government.

You've experienced the benefit of seeing tax deferred funds grow for you in a restrictive fashion. If you really want to make a difference in your grandchildren's' lives, make a contribution to their Roth IRA (assuming they meet the qualification requirements) which has penalties that could keep them invested until they reach retirement age. If you made a $2,000 contribution at their college graduation, by the time they reach age forty, and the funds were invested within a mutual fund that returned over eleven percent annually, they would have tax free proceeds available for them at their retirement of more than $130,000.

Now that is a way to leave a legacy.

2. Make Sure Your Documents are in Order

Another mistake made by many retirees is they assume that all of their retirement assets will automatically be transferred to their spouse upon their death. This is not the case. Each state may be different with regard to rules regarding the disbursement of assets.

In one such state, a lady in her second marriage was supporting her husband, by withdrawing assets from her IRA in order to take care of her husband who had been admitted to an assisted living home. He had been there for nearly two years. She never concerned herself with the review of her retirement documentation because she assumed that upon her death, her husband would receive the assets from her rather substantial IRA account, if something had happened to her. A problem arose when she died prematurely, and her retirement account listed her first husband as the beneficiary, leaving the current husband with no financial assistance for his care.

After her death, the current husband was transferred to a new assisted living home which accepted Medicaid recipients, while her first husband withdrew nearly $1.2 million from the deceased wife's IRA and purchased a new home in Florida.

Events such as these can be avoided. Never assume things that are yours will transfer to those who you love automatically. When it comes to laws surrounding retirement accounts, it's very important you take the time to verify that the loved ones in which you intend to receive your funds are actually listed as benefactors should something happen to you. There's no better time than the present to pick up the phone and request a copy of your beneficiary statement or confirm this with your financial professional or wherever your retirement assets are held.

3. Common Distribution Mistakes

There are typically two types of major mistakes when it comes to distributions from IRA accounts, In some cases, the distribution is a premature distribution in which the owner of the IRA assumes that since he retired at age 55, he's able to withdraw funds from his IRA without penalty. While this is partially true, there are certain rules which need to be followed in order to avoid the 10 percent penalty associated with early withdrawal.

In order to avoid the 10 percent penalty on the early withdrawal of IRA funds, several conditions must be met such as the funds to be used towards the purchase of your first home, medical expenses above seven and a half percent of your adjusted gross income, disability, or to pay qualified higher education expenses. In the case of early retirees, you may exercise rule 72(t) of the Internal Revenue code which allows you to take distributions prior to age 59 ½ assuming the following are met:

- Payments must continue to age 59 ½ or for 5 years—whichever is longer.

- Deviation from the payment schedule may result in an IRS penalty of 10% retroactively on all prior distributions.

- Taxpayers with multiple IRAs are not required to aggregate the accounts for purposes of calculating the substantially equal payments.

- Taxpayers can create a separate IRA account for pre-59 ½ withdrawals, allowing other accounts to grow undisturbed and tax-deferred.

Unfortunately there are some retirees do not have a financial professional to assist them in managing their qualified retirement accounts and they fail to withdraw the minimum mandatory distribution amount according to IRS guidelines.

When this occurs, the penalties could be very severe, as high as 50 percent of the amount you should have withdrawn.

Unfortunately this happens most frequently to individuals have several IRA accounts with different banks, mutual fund companies, and brokerage firms; because they believe it's better to have things spread out versus with one person. If you aren't able to keep up with taking distributions from these plans, it could cost you several thousands of dollars that you may never see again.

Here are a few more facts you should be aware of concerning your retirement accounts.

If you take money out of your traditional IRA before you are 59–1/2, you will always pay a penalty.

There are many ways to get money out of your IRA without paying a penalty. You can take the money in installments over your life expectancy no matter how young you are. You can also take money out for certain college expenses or to help buy a first home. Don't forget, however, that even if you are allowed to take money out of your traditional IRA without paying a penalty, you must still pay income tax on the money.

When you make withdrawals from your traditional IRA, you must take cash.

You are permitted to take "property" such as stock shares or corporate bonds out of your IRA instead of selling them first and taking the cash. This rule is helpful when you want to continue to hold certain securities.

You cannot change the beneficiary of your IRA after you turn 70–1/2.

You can always change your beneficiary. It's up to you to decide who gets your money after you die.

Every year after you turn 70–1/2, you are required to take money out of your 401(k).

If you continue to work past age 70–1/2, you are not required to take money out of your 401(k) until you actually retire, unless you are an owner of the business.

If you are 70–1/2, you are required to take money out of each IRA you own.

If you own several IRAs, a special rule allows you to total the amount that you are required to take from each IRA and then take the grand total from just one. Or you can take the total from several IRAs in any amounts you like. The IRS keeps tabs on the value of retirement accounts, so if you are taking one distribution from one of your IRA accounts that will cover your mandatory requirement, make sure you provide documentation to the IRS regarding the account the distribution took place. This could prevent you from receiving more letters from the IRS to explain your actions.

If your children are the beneficiaries of your 401(k) or other retirement plan, they can roll over the plan into their own IRA when you die.

A spouse is the only beneficiary who is allowed to roll over your retirement plan into his or her own IRA. No other beneficiary may do so, not even your children.

If your children are the beneficiaries of your IRA, they must take all the money out of the IRA immediately after you die and pay taxes on it.

With careful planning by you when you complete your IRA beneficiary form and by your children in the year after your death, your children should be able to spread distributions out over their own life expectancies.

No distributions are ever required from a Roth IRA.

Although you are not required to take distributions from your own Roth IRA during your lifetime, all beneficiaries except your spouse must begin taking distributions after you die.

If you convert your traditional IRA to a Roth IRA and then withdraw some or the entire converted amount in the next couple of years, those amounts could be subject to income tax.

Converted amounts are never subject to regular income tax after the year of conversion. You already paid the tax. However, they might be subject to an early withdrawal penalty if you take the money out too soon after the conversion and if you are younger than age 59–1/2.

Once you reach age 70–1/2, you must take a specific amount out of your IRA each year—no more, no less.

The amount that you are required to take out of your IRA after age 70–1/2 is a "minimum" required amount. You may take more, but you may not take less.

Retirement accounts may represent a large portion of your nest egg. It's important to have an understanding of the current tax laws so that your assets are not adversely impacted. It's also important that if your hope is to transfer these assets to loved ones or charities who could benefit from your gift, you've taken the necessary steps to ensure all documents have been completed to transfer assets directly to them without the government or IRS interfering. These are a few very important considerations you need to follow so that you and your family receive full benefit from your years of savings.

17

Do I Really Need Insurance?

I don't know of anyone who looks forward to writing checks to insurance companies on policies that may never needed, but unfortunately, as soon as we let a policy lapse, that's when we needed it the most.

Retirees always search for opportunities to lower the outgoing expenses to their budget and one consideration may be the elimination of insurance premiums, but before you allow that policy to lapse, there are several questions you need to ask yourself such as; if something happened to me or my spouse, how would it affect my Personal Retirement Road Map? Am I better to cancel a policy that I may never use and invest the funds somewhere else? My mother and father never spent any time in a nursing home, why do I need long term care insurance? These are legitimate questions with no appropriate answer, but one thing is certain, it's likely you will need some form of insurance to secure your retirement dreams.

Your family's history will play a large role in determining if you need cancer insurance, long term care insurance, or life insurance during retirement, but other forms of insurance coverage may depend on your personal financial situation. Some insurance coverage cannot be avoided such as medical. These types of coverage's should be a permanent fixture in your life just like any utility bill. There are some utilities you don't need such as cable or internet, but there are some utilities you need such as electricity, water, and telephone. Could you get by on less, sure, but insurance is protecting against the "what if's". Your retirement years will be filled with plenty of questions, with proper insurance many of the concerns will be addressed having the appropriate insurance.

What Type of Insurance Will I Need?

There are obvious areas where insurance is needed such as homeowners, automobile, dental and health to supplement Medicare or to cover your costs until you reach Medicare, but here is information on other forms of insurance which could play a vital role in your retirement future.

Long Term Care:

Long term care insurance is coverage that extends beyond acute care you may receive in a hospital. While many insurance providers will cover the cost of care while you are in the hospital, once you are released, and you still require additional care for disabilities or a chronic illness, the additional medical expenses such as nursing care or physical therapy may not be covered under your health plan.

Long term care insurance is generally used to cover the cost of care in a nursing home, assisted living homes and services, nurses or medical technicians who visit your home to provide care, assistants that help in your home with activities such as bathing, dressing, eating, and cleaning, or community programs that offer adult services for seniors.

Many retirees and seniors make the mistake to assume that their current health care plan, supplemental health insurance or disability policy, or Medicare will pay for long term care needs, this is simply not true. Most policies cover only the acute injury or illness, once you have been released, you are on your own to pay for your own recovery. Medicare A only covers skilled care, which in many cases means hospital care, thus it's estimated that Medicare covers roughly nine percent of those patients who are admitted into nursing homes in the first one hundred days, after one hundred days it's up to you to provide you own care insurance of rely on Medicaid which is different state to state.

According to the American Association of Home Services for the Aging about 69 percent of people who reach age 65 will need some form of long term care, whether in the form of a nursing home or assisted living in their lifetime. Once they reach the nursing home, their stay will average approximately 2 ½ years.

The average annual cost for a semi-private room in a nursing home facility is about $66,000 a year. If you had 24 hour care, that cost grew to more than $150,000 per year. The average increase in nursing home costs has grown about six percent a year over the past decade. According to the American Council of Life Insurers, the average cost of nursing home care could be as high as $110,000 a year by 2015 and rise to nearly $200,000 a year by 2030.

While no one enjoys paying insurance premiums, especially when they aren't used, the odds favor that at some point you or your spouse will need the assistance of a nursing home or assisted living home for your care. All of us would prefer to live in the best environment affordable, so unless you have the financial assets to cover your long term care needs, the sooner you choose to invest in a long term care policy, the better chance you have of obtaining an annual premium that your budget can afford.

Over the years several insurance companies have dropped long term care insurance coverage as an option to their customers. This disturbing trend signifies the issues insurance companies encounter in predicting long term care costs. As these companies decide to exit this type of business, people looking for coverage could be held hostage by just a few companies that could charge outrageous premiums for their protection.

If you feel you are a candidate for long term care insurance, here are some important points you want to keep in mind.

1. Use Strong Insurance Companies

It's unlikely that premiums will remain constant during the course of your life, but some companies such as John Hancock, MetLife, and Genworth have been in business for years and don't have a reputation of dramatically raising the premiums on their customers. Their premiums may be higher than some of their competitors, but it's important to stick with a company that can manage their long term care business in such a way where the premiums are affordable.

Make sure that any policy you purchase is qualified under the Health Insurance and Portability Act of 1996. This act allowed for the premiums to be tax deductible and to pay out tax free benefits. This information should be available from the company in which you are purchasing the policy.

As you consider an insurance carrier to cover your long term care, verify the carrier not only has the financial assets to cover your claims, but they have serviced long term care policies for more than five years. Some companies offer deals to consumers. These companies should be scrutinized. Consider the insurance rating of the company from agencies such as A.M. Best, Standard and Poor's, or Duff & Phelps. These rating agencies can be found online and can provide financial information on the insurance carrier and their ability to pay claims. You want a company that has solid financial strength in order to insure your benefits will be there when you need them. Higher ratings suggest consistent and predictable performance.

As you consider long term insurance, before you provide a check, ask for a sample contract from the carrier. A sample contract, while not specific, will provide you with general information as to the promises the insurance carrier is willing to offer. Do not depend on the insurance agent to provide you with verbal information. When it comes down to it, the insurance company will pay upon the stipulations within the contract. If a carrier isn't willing to provide you with a sample contract, this should be indication you should avoid the carrier.

Never make a check payable to the insurance agent. Always make your check payable to the insurance company who is issuing your policy. In many cases, most states will allow a grace period for you to review your policy and cancel it without a penalty. If you have not received your policy within 30 days of writing your check, contact your agent and the insurance company.

2. Determine How Much Per Day

Long term care policies typically provide coverage on a daily basis. For example, the coverage you choose may be for $100 per day or as much as $500 per day. Should you need to enact this policy, this amount will help determine the type of home or center you choose.

The cost of nursing homes or assisted living centers will vary from region to region. The cost in New York is likely to be higher versus Dalton, GA. Depending on your region and locale, you want to consider and visit all types of facilities when choosing your policy. You may find a center that is outside a metropolitan area where the cost of care is significantly lower and provide equal quality care if not higher.

3. Compare Policies

Each insurance company offers different discounts and variations of the type of coverage you can receive. For example, some companies have no waiting period before the policy is enacted, some offer a waiting period for a few months to see if your need is permanent or temporary. Some offer home care or assisted living as an option.

All of these options could directly affect your premium and coverage. You may look at all the alternatives that are available to you to see how you could perhaps lower your premium or maximize your coverage by making changes to your policy.

If your work offers long term care insurance, don't automatically sign up for their coverage. Depending on your health and needs, you could possibly get a better deal on your own, and your premium could be even lower if you include your spouse for coverage as well.

When you consider coverage, don't automatically go with the least expensive coverage. The popular phrase "You get what you pay for" is so true when considering long term care insurance. The last thing you want to do is to invest thousands of dollars over time with a company that suddenly falls into receivership with the state or goes bankrupt.

As you compare policies, you need to know if hospitalization is required. In some cases, long term care policies will only begin paying benefits after you've been treated at a hospital. You want to make sure your policy includes payment for impairment of any kind including the inability to perform activities from daily living.

Some companies will have a pre-existing condition clause. Avoid these companies which have these clauses in their contract. This is another reason why it's important to see a sample policy before you pay for insurance. Just because you had a heart ailment in the past does not give the insurance company the right to use this against you in the future when you may need the benefit for a stroke.

When you choose your policy, if you can't afford your premiums, make sure the insurance company will allow you to downgrade your coverage and retain the policy in place. The last thing you want to do is pay premiums for twenty years and not have the assurance that you'll be protected should conditions change in your life.

4. Inflation Protection

We just discussed the expected rising costs of nursing home care in the future. Why would you not consider adding a rider to protect you from these future increases?

Some policies offer you the opportunity to adjust your daily benefit annually in order to cover the rising costs of nursing home and assisted living centers. If they're costs rise 5 percent annually, you want to ensure that your long term care policy has a rider that allows for your $100 per day cost today, increases each year by a percentage similar to the rising cost of care in the industry. Some contracts will offer you $100 a day policy, and in twenty years when you need it, that's exactly what they will pay, $100 per day, when the actual cost for care has now grown to over $500 per day.

Other policies may offer you the opportunity to add additional coverage at a later date. This may be more suitable for a family who has not had several of their relatives enter nursing homes or assisted living centers. This option may lower the cost for care, especially if it's not needed.

5. Waiting Period

You have the option to choose how long you want to wait before you put the policy in force. Some policies start immediately, others could wait as long as a year before the policy starts paying. The longer the waiting period, the lower your premiums should be, but the longer the waiting period, the more that comes out of your personal investments.

When you choose an acceptable waiting period, make an assumption as to when you're likely to use the insurance. If you're 60 today, and your life expectancy is 85, assume you may need assisted living or nursing home care in about fifteen years. Every five years, you're likely to see the cost of nursing home and assisted living care rise about 50 percent for every $100. So in fifteen years, it's likely a $100 per day policy today, will need $250—$300. From this data, estimate how much of your personal savings you would be willing to spend in order to cover this cost.

The average waiting period most people use is 60 to 90 days. So if you choose a 90-day waiting period, this would mean that you could afford to use as much as $30,000 (in 2007 dollars) from your personal investments before your policy becomes in force. If you're not comfortable waiting that long, the annual premiums are likely to be a bit higher, and likewise you can lower your annual premiums by waiting to exercise the policy. This is a personal decision that you and your family should make in order to determine which is best suited for you based upon your needs and asset levels.

6. The Benefit Period

When you choose your policy, you also must choose how long your payments will be paid out. Benefit periods will often range from two years to your lifetime. Increasing the benefit period from three years to a lifetime could double your annual premium, so you need to consider this when choosing a policy. What is important to some people may not be important to you.

According to the Centers for Disease Control, the average nursing home stay is about two to three years, but these averages don't include people who are in a nursing home for just a few weeks after a hospital stay, others who are in a nursing home for a decade or more, and others who have home health care or assisted living needs.

As you consider choosing a benefit period, the difficulty will be to choose a period when your insurance will be there for you. If the average stay nursing home stay is about two and a half years, then a policy which carries a benefit period of three to five years makes sense, but you need to consider other factors such as family history. For example in my family, strokes are common on my side. My uncle spent twenty-five years in a home before his death. Other families may have a history of Alzheimer's which we know is a devastating disease not only on the individual, but also on the family. If your family has a history of Parkinson's or Multiple Sclerosis, you need to consider long term care.

If you happen to be one of those individuals with a family history of the following diseases in your family such as chronic memory loss, liver cirrhosis, muscular dystrophy, Parkinson's disease, Alzheimer's disease, senility or dementia, or multiple strokes, you may not even qualify for long term care insurance. Insurance companies today realize these diseases typically prolong life for an individual and may be very costly to the insurance company; therefore they could disqualify you even for a family history illness. If you have parents or grandparents who had these types of histories, you may be better to purchase insurance sooner rather than later.

7. Don't Skimp

Like many insurance contracts, the more options you add, the higher the cost you can expect for your coverage. Long Term care policies are no different. Some people prefer Cadillac's; others do just as well driving Chevrolets. It really depends on your personal preference, family history, and the cost to ensure your assets.

Make sure your long term coverage has a *home rider* attached to it. Many companies will offer coverage, only as it relates to nursing home care. Medicaid for example in many states does not offer home health care for those who can no longer stay in the hospital. Some key services that are provided under the home rider include cooking, shopping, changing beds, cleaning the house and doing laundry. Not all policies riders provide coverage for homemaker services and some require that they be specifically included in a plan of care. Look for policies that clearly define these services and provide you with a choice.

We've all heard the horror stories of what happens to other seniors inside nursing homes and statistics bear out that recovery times and quality of life is far better if we can remain within the comfort of our own homes versus a nursing home, but if you want to recover from home, you need to make sure your long term care policy provides benefits to be paid to providers who take care of you.

8. Tax and Other Considerations

Under the Health Insurance Portability and Accountability Act, also known as *Kennedy-Kassebaum*, passed in 1996, qualified long-term care insurance policies receive special tax treatment. To be considered "qualified", policies issued on or after January 1, 1997, must adhere to regulations established by the National Association of Insurance Commissioners adopted in January 1993. Among the requirements are that the policy must offer the consumer the options of "inflation" and "nonforfeiture" protection, although the consumer can choose not to purchase these features.

The policies must also offer both activities of daily living (ADL) and cognitive impairment triggers, but may not offer a medical necessity trigger. "Triggers" are conditions that must be present for a policy to be activated. Under the ADL trigger, benefits may begin only when the beneficiary needs assistance with at least two of six ADLs. The ADLs are: eating, toileting, transferring, bathing, dressing or continence. In addition, a licensed health care practitioner must certify that the need for assistance with the ADLs is reasonably expected to continue for at least ninety days. Under a cognitive impairment trigger, coverage begins when the individual has been certified to require substantial supervision to protect him or her from threats to health and safety due to cognitive impairment.

Benefits from reimbursement policies, which pay for the actual services a beneficiary receives, are not included in income. Benefits from per diem or indemnity policies, which pay a predetermined amount each day, are not included in income except amounts that exceed the beneficiary's total qualified long-term care expenses or $250 per day (in 2006), whichever is greater.

9. Assets

Every parent always considers leaving a legacy behind for their family. In many instances, their parents left something behind for them, and they want to leave something behind for their family, but a stay in a nursing home could drain most of the assets before that opportunity arises.

As we mentioned earlier, it's important to consider family history as a key determinant whether you should consult long term care policies. Another key determinant will be the amount of assets you have to draw from in case you would require nursing home assistance in the future. Several experts have their own opinion as to how much is enough, but several have agreed that if you have a house, car, and less than $75,000 in liquid assets (savings, IRA's, etc), then you should not consider purchasing a long term care policy. The cost to cover a two to three year stay in the nursing home would not be worth the additional premiums you would pay over time.

Likewise if you have a liquid net worth of $3 million or more, it does not make sense to purchase long term care insurance, simply because a similar stay in the nursing home would not have a material impact on your financial well being.

10. When Do I Purchase Long Term Care Insurance?

Unfortunately most retirees will fit somewhere in between of having more than $75,000 in assets and less than $3 million in assets which means most retirees should have long term care insurance. As our life expectancy continues to increase, so to will the demands of healthcare coverage.

According to various insurance companies, the best time to purchase long term care insurance is between the ages of 50 to 60 depending on your health and your family's history. The premiums are usually low during this period and become more affordable. The American Association of Homes and Services for the aging indicates that the average annual cost for long term care insurance is approximately $1,337.00 for individuals under age 65, but the average cost of long term care insurance over age 65 is nearly $2,500.00.

If you haven't purchased long term care insurance and you are planning to retire, buy coverage immediately. I understand you won't be happy with another bill impacting your retirement budget, but would you consider eliminating auto insurance? It's a similar type of risk. You may never have had an accident your entire life, but when it happens, and someone is hurt, aren't you appreciative you have the coverage? Research various policies, companies, and features of long term care insurance and find the right policy for you and your family.

If you're over age 70, at this point I don't believe long term care insurance is a prudent expense. As with many insurance policies, once you reach a certain age, you become a risk to the insurance company and they need to protect the company. Remember, insurance companies are in the business of hoping the "what ifs" never occur.

Once you've reached age 70 you may find the cost of coverage isn't worth the potential cost of two to three years of nursing home coverage. This is not to say that depending on where you live long term care coverage isn't affordable to you, but consider the annual cost of nursing home coverage today and for the next three years, and equate that to the potential cost of premiums over an extended period of time. If the cost is worth the benefit, you may want to consider coverage.

Many retirees today see the cost of long term care and it's understandable why it's such a hard decision to implement the cost into their retirement budget. With so few companies offering coverage, the cost for many of these policies are high. It's important that you consider long term care for your family as soon as possible, even if you begin with a small daily benefit amount. Many companies offer rebates if the policy is never used, similar to whole life insurance policies, but unless you've had family who have lived years in nursing homes, you can never appreciate the value of insurance until you actually see it at work.

Long Term Care Partnership Policies

Many middle-income people have too many assets to qualify for Medicaid but can't afford a pricey long-term care insurance policy. Four states—California, Connecticut, Indiana and New York—offer special long-term care policies that can allow buyers to protect assets and qualify for Medicaid when the long-term care policy runs out. These are called "partnership policies," and they are intended to provide incentives for people to purchase long-term care insurance policies that will cover at least some of their long-term care needs. (Note: A fifth state, Illinois has a partnership program, which is technically still in effect, but few or no policies are being sold.)

In California and Connecticut, the asset protection offered by partnership policies is dollar-for-dollar: for every dollar of coverage that your long-term care policy provides you can keep a dollar in assets that normally would have to be spent down to qualify for Medicaid. So, for example, if you're single, you would normally be allowed only $2,000 in assets in order to qualify for Medicaid coverage of long-term care. But if you buy a long-term care insurance policy that provides $150,000 in benefits, you would be allowed to retain $152,000 in assets and still qualify for Medicaid. (These states set limits on the assets that can be protected.)

In New York, the partnership policy benefits are even more significant. Once you have exhausted the benefits from your long-term care partnership policy, you can qualify for Medicaid coverage no matter your level of assets. In other words, an unlimited amount of assets can be protected.

Indiana offers either of the above models, depending on when the policy was purchased and the policy's design.

Bear in mind that the Medicaid asset protection will only work if you receive your long-term care in the state where you bought the policy, or in another partnership state that has a reciprocal agreement with the first state.

Disability

If you're a retiree and you rely upon the additional income you earn each month from your job, you may want to consider disability insurance.

Disability policies are usually purchased to replace a portion of your regular income (usually about 60 percent) when you incur an accident or injury. In many cases you can short disability insurance is provided or available from your employers insurance, but when your employer does not offer coverage, you may need to consider an outside agency.

If an accident occurs while you're on the job, it's likely that your employer's workman's compensation insurance will cover not only your medical bills, but compensate you for time away from work. It's important to make sure that the employer you choose has workman's compensation insurance. Many states today require insurance for employees, but it's a good question to ask as you consider a part-time job.

If you are injured for more than twelve months, you may be eligible to receive Social Security Benefits. Workman's Compensation usually covers a period of time until you are able to come back and fulfill your job or a similar job within a certain period of time. If after twelve months you are not able to perform these duties due to a disability, then you could apply for Social Security disability benefits. If you receive Workman's Compensation payments, these payments may offset how much Social Security benefits you may receive.

In some situations there may be times when the employer offers sick leave and vacation time. According to the Family Medical Leave Laws, if you are an employee that has worked more than 1250 hours for a company, you may use your sick and vacation pay to subsidize time you may take off where the Family Medical Leave Act is exercised. For this act to be in place, your employer must have at least 50 employees working for him. The law allows a worker to take up to twelve weeks during a twelve month period of time for a serious health condition.

If you find yourself needing income in order to make ends meet, and none of these conditions apply to you, it may be in your best interest to participate in a short term disability program with your employer's group plan or purchase a policy on your own. Some retirees make the mistake of assuming the social security benefits will replace your lost salary, but in reality social security will only replace a limited portion of your salary and the requirements to receive the benefits are very strict.

As you consider a short term disability policy, here are some key points to remember. Make sure that your policy cannot be cancelled and that it may be renewed every year as long as you make your premium payments on time. Another point to remember is if the policy premiums appear to be expensive, consider having lower premiums in the beginning years of your policy and higher premiums as the years go on. The reason for this is simply the likelihood that after a few years, you may find yourself in a position where you don't need to work, so the need for a short term disability policy may be mute.

To get an idea of how much this added insurance may cost, you can go online and find numerous sites that can provide you with quotes as to what you could expect a policy to cost. Take the time to do some simulations before you sit down and meet with an insurance representative. You may be able to use your quote as a bargaining chip in order to lower your premium amount. Don't forget to ask for a discount especially if your insurance representative handles other insurance needs such as life, home, car, or long term care.

Life Insurance

I'm not devoting a lot of time on life insurance simply because by the time you get to a level where you are retired, the life insurance you owned while you raised your family has served its purpose. You've successfully raised your kids, built your nest egg, and now it's time to reap the rewards. Why spend much needed income on something you may never need?

I believe that depending on your asset level, the ownership of life insurance when you are retired may be a subjective attitude. Some people simply feel they must have life insurance. Others wonder if it may be useful to their children in the future. Whatever the reason, you need to make the decision as to whether you keep it or not. It was always intended to be there for your spouse if something happened to you during your working years. Now that you're no longer working, perhaps it has outlived its purpose.

There are two basic types of insurance coverage, term, which will pay benefits as long as you die within a specified period of time (the least expensive) and permanent, which provides coverage as long as you continue to make contributions or have built enough "cash value" so that the dividends provided by the insurance product are enough to pay for the insurance coverage.

Which of these policies is suited for you depends upon your personal situation. Many insurance representatives will suggest you use permanent insurance as an option because it allows you to take any cash value out over a period of time. I do not believe that insurance should be used as a form of investment, so before you consider whether you need life insurance, here are some quick questions to ask:

What is the insurance to be used for?
Do I have debts that will need to be paid upon my death?
Will my spouse have enough income to survive comfortably the remainder of her life?
Do I have enough assets to bury myself and my wife?
When I die, will most of my assets go to my family or the government?
Do I want to provide a legacy for my grandchildren that are not part of my estate?

These are important questions that can help steer you in a direction as to whether you need life insurance.

Umbrella Policies/Liability Policies

Depending on the coverage you have on your current auto, home, property, or business liability insurance, an Umbrella Insurance Policy may be necessary.

The purpose of an Umbrella policy is to "shelter" your assets from continued claims once the initial coverage of your original policy that was affected has been exhausted. These types of policies are especially helpful for individuals who have a large amount of assets that could be exposed if the wrong situation arose.

Another purpose of the Umbrella policy is to cover those "unforeseen" events such as; your dog running out and biting a child on the cheek, or your mail carrier falling on a crack on your driveway as he brings you a package for your signature, or an auto accident where someone has died.

A basic Umbrella policy could cost a few hundred dollars per year, but provide you with peace of mind in knowing you're covered.

What is important to remember is that insurance premiums are a budgetary expense that needs to be included in your annual budget. Many people forget that some of these premiums are paid on a semi annual basis and are never factored into their household expenses. You should treat these expenses just as you would a utility. They will be a necessary item that you may need to rely upon in the future.

More information about insurance recommendations for retirees may be founding by searching Google, or visiting www.aarp.org. Please remember that many of these websites are in the business to sell you insurance. Use their resources and information to determine if you are a candidate for coverage, then meet with your personal financial advisor or insurance agent to discuss your coverage needs in detail.

18

Planning Your Estate

While some may want to live forever, death can be worse for those who choose to procrastinate when it comes to planning their legacy. It's likely that you've had thoughts concerning your own death and the legacy you would like to leave behind. You may have taken the necessary steps in your youth to have the necessary legal documents drafted to protect your family, but now is a good time to make sure the legal documents you have are up to date as it relates to current federal and state estate tax laws.

Estate planning is for everyone! It doesn't matter how large or small your estate may be. It is important that you prepare a plan so your loved ones benefit from the gifts you may leave behind.

Estate planning isn't costly and is very easy to complete. It simply requires you to sit down with those who are close to you and determine how your legacy should be shared. In many cases, estate planning starts with a last will and testament which outlines a broad structure as to how your assets should be shared, but proper estate planning is much more than this. A proper estate plan will encompass more than a will; it includes several documents which can protect you and your family. The cost and time you take to draft these documents is minimal compared to the burden you could place on your family.

There are three important estate planning documents that every retiree should consider, they are: a durable power of attorney, a living will or healthcare proxy, and a will or trust.

The first, a durable power of attorney is a document designed to managing your property during your life, in case you are ever unable to do so yourself. The second, a living will or healthcare proxy is a document designed to communicate with the medical profession as to your wishes should become incapacitated during your life, and the third document, a will or trust is used to express your intentions with regard to the disbursement of your assets at your death. These three documents are necessities for basic estate planning. They may be as broad as specific as you like and you may make amendments to them as the years go by.

Today many retirees utilize other estate planning documents to ensure more of their assets go to their designees rather than the government. To determine if you may need additional documents to protect your estate, you should seek the counsel of a qualified estate planning attorney or tax attorney who can analyze your estate and provide recommendations to further protect your estate.

If you're one of those individuals who haven't taken the time to think about estate planning, this chapter is for you. The next few pages will highlight the three key components to any estate plan and how they work together to protect you and your family.

Durable Power of Attorney

In some cases a Durable Power of Attorney may be the most important estate planning document you create. A Durable Power of Attorney is a legal document that allows you to appoint a trusted individual as your *attorney in fact*. This person primarily oversees your financial affairs should you become incapacitated for various reasons.

A Durable Power of Attorney can be as broad or as specific as you make it out to be. You may choose to have your attorney in fact represent you with regard to writing checks to pay bills, or make deposits into your bank account. You may choose to give your attorney in fact more power by providing him with the power to act for you with regard to business decisions, manage your investments, or file your tax returns. Whatever the stipulations may be, this document can provide specific language that informs creditors, banks, and vendors that the attorney in fact is acting on your behalf.

The document will become binding as soon as it is signed and will remain in effect if you become incapacitated or until you die. You may rescind the power of attorney at any time which also makes the person whom you've named as the attorney in fact someone which you can trust completely. Remember you are authorizing someone to act on your behalf which has the same power as you. The person you designate needs to be carefully considered. They should be individuals who may have a vested interest in your health, transfer of your assets, or your love. Depending on who you select, a qualified attorney will be able to provide you with the necessary information in order to draft a document that is specific to your requests so that your *attorney in fact* may execute your wishes at the appropriate time.

Living Wills/Healthcare Proxy/Healthcare Durable Power of Attorney

As modern medicine continues to prolong human lives, it could influence your life if you become incapacitated or unable to feed yourself. Living wills and healthcare proxies were created for these circumstances.

When you sit down and take the time to work with a personal attorney to create a will, you need to take this time and have your attorney include a medical directive that will provide information to the medical staff and the courts as to the conditions in which you do not wish medical support should you become unavailable to make these decisions on your own.

There is a clear difference between what a health care proxy and a healthcare durable power of attorney can do for you versus a living will. A healthcare proxy and healthcare durable power of attorney provides a personal representative that you choose to make decisions on your behalf that could affect you medically. This document is usually in force when you are unconscious. The purpose of the personal representative is to weigh decisions based upon information provided by the medical staff, and make a decision as to whether they should continue medical care, perform a surgery, or provide another form of care. The document will become in force when the medical staff deems that you are not capable of interaction.

A living will is your written expression of how you want to be treated in certain medical conditions. Depending on state law, this document may permit you to express whether or not you wish to be given life-sustaining treatments in the event you are terminally ill or injured, and to give other medical directions that impact the end of life. Life-sustaining treatment simply means the use of available medical machinery and techniques, such as heart-lung machines, ventilators, and other medical equipment and techniques that will sustain and possibly extend your life, but which will not by themselves cure your condition. In addition to terminal illness or injury situations, most states permit you to express your preferences as to treatment using life-sustaining equipment and/or tube feeding for medical conditions that leave you permanently unconscious and without detectable brain activity.

A living will applies in situations where the decision to use such treatments may prolong your life for a limited period of time and not obtaining such treatment would result in your death. It does not mean that medical professionals would deny you pain medications and other treatments that would relieve pain or otherwise make you more comfortable. Living wills do not determine your medical treatment in situations that do not affect your continued life, such as routine medical treatment and non life-threatening medical conditions.

One of the issues with living wills is the determination as to whether you can recover from your condition in the future. This determination is usually left up to your attending physician and another doctor who has examined you. Most states permit you to include other medical directions that you wish your physicians to be aware of regarding the types of treatment you do or do not wish to receive. As you draft your will, you will want to provide as much specificity about those conditions in which your life should not be prolonged. Depending on the states, the courts could interfere with the broadness of the living will, and continue life support treatments. This could have devastating effects on your family as assets are needed to pay for extended care.

Because of many of these uncertainties you may want to consider a healthcare proxy or healthcare durable power of attorney along with a living will. This document will authorize someone you trust, in many cases not a family member, to make healthcare decisions for you if you are incapacitated. While you may only be unconscious, it allows for another individual to act as a surrogate on your behalf when making medical decisions that could affect your life. The reason that family members are not chosen is due to the emotional bond and situation that may be present. By choosing a trusted advisor, their mental capacity may not be impacted by your incapacitation.

Before confusion sets in as to whether you have a living will or a healthcare proxy, provide a copy of these documents to your personal physician, attorney, and the designee who has power of attorney over you. Make sure that each one of these individuals knows where the original documents have been placed or filed.

Another consideration is to carry a card in your wallet that indicates that you have a living will or healthcare proxy along with the name and the phone numbers of the designated decision maker who is capable of making decisions on your behalf.

Finally, place the phone number in the directory of your cell phone that says ICE (In Case of Emergency), EMERGENCY #, or CALL EMERG in order to provide medical providers or emergency crews with a number to call should you become incapacitated.

Wills

"The only sure thing in life is death and taxes" Benjamin Franklin

While you may think that upon your death you have finally relieved yourself of paying taxes to the government, depending on the amount of assets you own in your name, your estate may have to pay more in estate taxes than you've ever paid to the Federal Government in income taxes during your lifetime.

In many cases estate taxes will need to be paid to the government in addition to income taxes. It's amazing that even though you may have died; your family is still responsible for preparing an income tax return for you.

Federal estate taxes have historically been very expensive. Over the past few years Congress has been debating as to the amount of taxes should be paid based upon the assets you've attained over your lifetime. The tax rate applied to estates has reached a levy as high as 55 percent. These taxes have been especially hard on families who own farms or small businesses, where the owner has put blood sweat and tears into a business that has taken care of his family for many years, but now, must be sold in order to pay estate taxes.

Federal law allows descendants of the deceased nine months to pay estate tax levies to the government. While most individuals are allowed exemptions under the current revenue code which will eliminate the need for estate taxes to be paid, there are cases where the family must sell assets in order to pay estate taxes. In unfortunate cases, real property such as real estate, homes, businesses, or personal property must be sold in order to pay the taxes. No one is happy with government looking for their share but there are ways in which you could substantially reduce or eliminate potential estate taxes through proper planning.

One of the simpler ways to reduce or eliminate your estate taxes is to first take advantage of the estate tax exemption the government offers. This exemption amount will vary for future generations to come, based upon 2006-2008 guidelines, married couples could shelter up to $2 million dollars of assets from federal estate taxes. This can be easily done by transferring assets so that each spouse is a sole owner of a portion of the property you own together. For example, you could move the home into your wife's name, annuities, and other investment assets while you retain ownership of a retirement account or property.

Wills are the most common estate planning tool that many retirees will utilize. Unless you have an estate which is valued at more than a million dollars (including house, assets, cars, etc), you can protect most of your estate planning needs through what is called an *A-B will*. Wills for the most part are a legal document which explains how you would like your assets shared amongst your loved ones when you pass. In many cases, couples establish A-B wills, where if one spouse should die, the assets of the deceased spouse will transfer to the living spouse, but upon the death of the last surviving spouse, this is where a will could present problems.

Estate tax laws have changed dramatically over the years and it's important that you or a trusted advisor is aware of your personal asset base and keeps you abreast of potential changes in the tax laws and the impact it could have on your estate. In many cases you will meet with these individuals on an annual basis and it's a perfect time to discuss if any changes need to be addressed with your current estate plan. The small amount of time you spend communicating with these individuals could save your family a great deal of headaches and money.

A will can be as specific or as broad as you intend it to be. A will does not need to be specific. You can simply state that each child is to share in the total estate, but if you prefer to be more specific, a will can be as specific as you need it to be. Unfortunately some of the biggest disputes over wills take place over some of the smallest issues. In some cases, it's not the amount of assets in the bank that are split amongst siblings, but personal property or mementos that one child felt they deserved. If there are certain tangible items that are held in your estate that you want to go to a specific sibling, you should consider giving these items to your children before you pass, or at least have the items mentioned in the will in order to prevent infighting.

As you prepare your will, you will need to name a *personal representative* or an *executor* to oversee the disbursement of your estate. A personal representative or executor is charged by the court to execute the instructions of the will. It's important that the person you name be someone who you believe will not only be alive to execute these wishes, but someone who has your confidence. In many cases the executor of the will is a child. If you do not name an executor, then the court could name the first interested party who applies for the position.

Wills are necessary in order to provide a smooth transition through probate. If you die intestate (without a will), then the court will take the responsibility to perhaps name an executor for you or appoint a local attorney to oversee the disbursement of the assets and payment of taxes. The fees that would be charged for this action could be very high, thus cutting into the heirs proceeds.

Wills may be amended at any time prior to their filing with the courts or your death. You may find yourself in a position where you would like to change a portion of the will. This is a simple transaction that will require an amendment to your current will. The best recommendation would be to consult with the attorney who drafted your original will and request the necessary changes.

You may question whether you could file your own will without the assistance of attorney. The answer to this is yes. There are several online websites that now provide detailed information as to how this can be done, but during these times of changing tax laws, it may be in your best interest to work with an estate attorney who makes it his business to keep up with tax law changes and the potential impact it may have on his clients. By staying on his mailing list, you may gain invaluable information that could be beneficial to your heirs and your estate.

Now that we've discussed the three primary estate planning documents that every retiree should have, let's look at other documents which could benefit your personal situation.

Trusts

The word trust has different connotations for every person. For some it's a feeling of security, for others, it's a feeling of restriction. Years ago trusts were created for the protection of assets from the government and families. Trusts have a connotation of complex legal documents which contained many restrictions. For many years, the only institution which managed trusts were banks, and their fees they charged to manage these trusts were very expensive, but today, things are much different.

When more planning is needed to have more assets flow to family members and not to the government in the form of estate taxes, the creation of a *trust* could be a very cost effective method to utilize. The creation of a trust can offer several advantages depending on your situation. One of the best known benefits behind establishing a trust is the ability to avoid probate upon death. Unlike a will, when assets are placed into a trust, any property in the trust prior to the donor's death passes immediately to the beneficiaries by the terms of the trust without requiring probate. This can save time and money for the beneficiaries.

Another benefit behind the creation of a trust is for tax advantage reasons which benefit the donor and the beneficiary. These are often referred to as *credit shelter* or *life insurance* trusts. Other trusts may be used to protect property from creditors or to help the donor qualify for Medicaid. Unlike wills, trusts are private documents and only those individuals with a direct interest in the trust need know of trust assets and distribution. Provided they are well-drafted, another advantage of trusts is their continuing effectiveness even if the donor dies or becomes incapacitated.

Trusts fall into two basic categories: testamentary and inter vivos. A testamentary trust is one created by your will, and it does not come into existence until you die. In contrast, an inter vivos trust starts during your lifetime. You create it now and it exists during your life.

There are primarily two kinds of inter vivos trusts: *revocable* and *irrevocable*.

Revocable Trusts

Revocable trusts are often referred to as living trusts. With a revocable trust, the donor maintains complete control over the trust and may amend, revoke or terminate the trust at any time. This means that you, the donor, can take back the funds you put in the trust or change the trust's terms. Thus, the donor is able to reap the benefits of the trust arrangement while maintaining the ability to change the trust at any time prior to death.

Revocable trusts are generally used for the following purposes:

Asset management— They permit the named trustee to administer and invest the trust property for the benefit of one or more beneficiaries.

Avoiding probate— At the death of the person who created the trust, the *grantor* or *donor*, the trust property passes to whoever is named in the trust. It does not come under the jurisdiction of the probate court and its distribution need not be held up by the probate process. However, the property of a revocable trust will be included in the grantor's estate for tax purposes.

Tax planning—The assets of a revocable trust will be included in the grantor's taxable estate; the trust can be drafted so that the assets will not be included in the estates of the beneficiaries, thus avoiding taxes when the beneficiaries die.

Irrevocable Trusts

Irrevocable trusts are more permanent trusts and are designed not to be broken. In most circumstances, an irrevocable trust cannot be changed or amended by the donor. Property or assets placed into the trust may only be distributed by the trustee as provided for in the trust document itself. For instance, the donor may set up a trust under which he or she will receive income earned on the trust property, but that bars access to the trust principal. This type of irrevocable trust is a popular tool for Medicaid planning.

Some examples of irrevocable trusts include:

Testamentary Trusts— A testamentary trust is a trust created by a will. Such a trust has no power or effect until the will of the donor is probated. Although a testamentary trust will not avoid the need for probate and will become a public document as it is a part of the will, it can be useful in accomplishing other estate planning goals. For instance, the testamentary trust can be used to reduce estate taxes on the death of a spouse or provide for the care of a disabled child.

Supplemental Needs Trusts—The purpose of a supplemental needs trust is to enable the donor to provide for the continuing care of a disabled spouse, child, relative or friend. The beneficiary of a well-drafted supplemental needs trust will have access to the trust assets for purposes other than those provided by public benefits programs. In this way, the beneficiary will not lose eligibility for benefits such as Supplemental Security Income, Medicaid and low-income housing. A supplemental needs trust can be created by the donor during life or be part of a will.

Credit Shelter Trusts—Credit shelter trusts are a way to take full advantage of the estate tax exemption. The first two million dollars (under current 2007 federal estate tax guidelines) of an estate are exempt from taxes, so theoretically a husband and wife would have no estate tax if their estate is less than four million dollars. However, if one spouse dies and leaves everything to the surviving spouse, the surviving spouse may have an estate that is greater than two million dollars. When the surviving spouse dies, any part of the estate over two million dollars will be subject to estate tax.

To avoid this problem, the spouses can create a credit shelter trust as part of their estate plan. When one spouse passes away, the first two million dollars of that spouse's estate is put in to a trust. The surviving spouse can receive income from the trust, but as long as he or she does not control the principal, the money will not be included in the surviving spouse's estate when he or she passes away.

These are just a few examples of the types of trusts that are available to help you manage your assets and provide income for the duration of your life. One important fact about all trusts is that they will require proper execution which not only means the documents are in order, but that all parties, including a third party, that sign the trust must have the legal capacity and competence to understand the newly created trust and the ultimate effect on their estate or assets. If the person or the third party does not have the competence of how this trust could affect his estate or assets, then it could be voided in the future by potential lawsuits.

Irrevocable Life Insurance Trust

One way to remove life insurance from your estate is to name an irrevocable life insurance trust as the owner of the life insurance policy. An *ILIT* allows you to transfer current or new insurance policies into an irrevocable trust in which you are not an owner. According to the current Internal Revenue code, as long as you live for three years after the transfer of an existing life insurance policy, the death benefits may not be included in your estate and the proceeds are to be used according to the trust document. In many cases ILIT's are used to provide assets to children after estate taxes have been paid, fund charities, or create foundations.

Usually the ILIT is also the beneficiary of the policy, giving you the option of keeping the proceeds in the trust for years, with periodic distributions to your spouse, children and grandchildren. Proceeds kept in the trust may be protected from irresponsible spending and creditors, even ex-spouses.

Charitable Remainder Trust

A *Charitable Remainder Trust* or CRT's allow you to take highly appreciable assets such as stocks, businesses, or real estate and move these assets into a trust in order to receive lifetime income without paying any capital gains tax when these assets are sold. The benefit of a charitable remainder trust is two fold. The first benefit allows you to name a charity or charities to be a recipient of the assets within the trust upon the final death of you or your spouse. A second benefit is due to your gift to these charities, you will receive a reduced tax on the lifetime income you receive from this trust and a reduction in your taxable estate.

Charitable Remainder Trusts are very popular with retirees who do not have children or have children or have substantial assets in which they would like to designate a charity to receive. During your life, the trust would pay you income, and upon the death of the last owner of the trust, the charity would receive the proceeds of the trust.

Some retirees don't mind gifting assets to a charity upon their death, especially when the thought of receiving tax free from the value of these assets is so appealing, but what happens if conditions change. What happens if the retiree needs more than the income from the trust? Most CRT's are written today in such a way that should you need to delve into the trust for additional assets in order to maintain your standard of living, you are perfectly within your right. Remember, the assets go to the charity only after the owner or owners have passed, but there may be tax consequences from doing so since most of the assets placed into the trust were not taxed with capital gains. Before you decide to do this, you should consult with your attorney or tax attorney for current rules with regard to CRT trusts.

Charitable Lead Trusts

The *Charitable Lead Trust* while the name may be confused with charitable remainder trust shares no commonality; in fact, they operate in nearly an opposite fashion. The charitable lead trust (CLT) allows the owner to transfer assets into the trust which reduces your overall estate and saves your family from paying estate taxes, but instead of having the trust pay income to you, it pays income to a charity or charities you designate for a number of years or until you die. After the death of the owner or owners, the trust assets will revert back to the children or other beneficiaries you've named in your estate in many cases free from estate taxes.

While wills, trusts, and other legal documents may make your head spin and cause confusion as to which one is right for you, there are some other actions you could consider which would facilitate the flow you're your assets to your family instead of Uncle Sam

Qualified Personal Residence Trust

A qualified personal resident trust could you save estate taxes by removing your home from your estate now and allows you to continue to live in the house. In essence, here's how it works:

You transfer your home to a trust for a period of time, usually 10 to 15 years. During this time, you continue to live in your home. When the time it up, it transfers to the trust beneficiaries, usually your children. If you wish to stay there longer, you make arrangements to "pay rent". If you die before the trust ends, your home will be included in your estate, just as it would without a Qualified Personal Residence Trust.

The Qualified Personal Residence Trust leverages your estate tax exemption. Since your children won't receive the house until the trust ends, its value as a gift is reduced. For example, if the current value of your home is $250,000 and you put in a Qualified Personal Residence Trust for 15 years, its value for tax purposes could be as small as $75,000. That leaves much more of your qualified exemption for other assets.

Other Considerations

Some other forms of estate planning tools that could benefit your estate or your family include:

Family Limited Partnerships or Limited Liability Corporations

These entities allow you to reduce estate taxes by transferring assets such as farms, real estate holdings, a family business, or other investments to your children while you are alive and m maintain control.

Family LLP's or LLC's are becoming more popular with retirees. By setting up one of these, you're able to transfer assets into another entity in exchange for ownership interest. Even though you have a fiduciary responsibility to other owners, you control the LLP or LLC as a general partner or manager, and you give ownership interests to your children, which removes the value from your taxable estate.

The ownership interests are cannot be sold or transferred without your approval so this prevents your children from having assets leave due to divorce or unforeseen circumstances, and because there is no market value for your "interest" in the LLP or LLC since you're a manager or partner, the value of the assets are discounted.

In essence an LLP or LLC allows you to transfer your assets to your children without losing control of them.

Gifting

This is one of the simplest ways to transfer assets out of your estate and directly to your children and it doesn't require any legal meetings or documents. Each year the federal government allows individuals to gift up to $12,000 per year or $24,000 (as of 2007) if married to as many people as you choose. If you had three children and seven grandchildren, each year you could give as much as $240,000 in cash, stock, real estate, business ownership, or some other asset as a couple, to people who you would like to benefit with the exception of charities. Charities are not restricted by the amount of your gift.

You could give more, but it will eat into your estate tax exemption. The reason for this is because when both spouses give, it's considered a combined gift and estate tax exemption. While you're living, it's a gift tax exemption; after you die, it's an estate tax exemption, so while you may consider this option, there are some strings attached which is discussed in another chapter.

Insurance

No one likes insurance but it could serve a purpose in estate planning. If you are in good health and recently retired, you may consider insurance as a way to replace an asset given to a charity, provide a gift to children or grandchildren, or provide funds to pay estate taxes. There are rules as it relates to the tax free benefit of insurance upon the death of an individual. In most cases you do not want to be the owner of the policy, but perhaps one of your children or an Irrevocable Life Insurance Trust.

Debate continues to build as to the benefits of purchasing life insurance once many of your goals have been reached in retirement. Some may argue that purchasing life insurance could provide a financial legacy for your family or spouse; others will argue the cost of insurance isn't practical when you may be living on a fixed income. Both sides provide valid arguments, but what matters is whether the purchase of life insurance fits as it relates to the goals and dreams you've outlined in your Personal Retirement Road Map. Before you consider life insurance, consult with those individuals who can provide additional information such as your attorney, your tax advisor and financial partner.

While estate planning may not immediately affect your plans for or during retirement, it will need to be addressed at some point in the future. Over the years many retirees have focused on looking just a few years ahead without considering the obstacles that could face them in the future. If retirees do not take estate planning seriously, they could be providing for the government rather than their family or charities.

Don't let the information in this chapter overwhelm you. For many retirees estate planning will simply encompass the three major documents mentioned earlier in this chapter: a durable power of attorney, a living will or healthcare proxy, and a will. Depending where you are on your journey through retirement, your Personal Retirement Road Map will dictate what steps you need to take now in order to protect your family from government invasion of your assets.

If you happen to be in a position where current estate laws could negatively impact your estate or other conditions exist where you would like to leave a legacy for your heirs, now is the time to plan and meet with a qualified estate planning attorney or tax attorney who specializes in estate planning. Many of these attorneys will provide you a free consultation to determine if you are comfortable with his abilities, but before you go, take the time to write down some questions you need answers to, and take the time to write down in layman's terms, how you picture your family and your assets being protected. Some of the key questions you would want to know include:

What is your fee to establish a proper estate plan for my family?
What does this fee cover?
How do you communicate with your clients with regard to changes in the tax law? Is it my responsibility to contact you, or do you contact me?
What is your charge for additional consultations?
If I have an estate tax issue which requires me to go to court who will defend me?

For more information on how to select and locate an attorney who specializes in estate planning, you may want to consult with a friend, associate, or other family member as to referrals they can provide. If no one has a recommendation to offer you can visit http://www.search-attorneys.com for attorneys in your city and state that specialize in estate planning services.

19

Giving

As humans, it's in our nature to nurture and care for our offspring and others who may have had a positive impact on our life. In years past you may have benefited from an aunt, uncle, grandparent, or parent that passed financial assets to you. You may find yourself in a fortunate situation where you have accumulated so much; you may not have a need for some of your assets. If this is the case, you may begin to think about your legacy and the ways you could make a difference in someone's life, thus the question could arise, *when do you give?*

The only way you will be able to determine when it's appropriate to begin gifting your assets to your heirs or other interested parties is to review your Personal Retirement Road Map and decide if your assets are to a place where you can afford to give them away. Think about it this way. You've planned a cross country trip from New York to California to see relatives you haven't seen in years. Your budget is $5,000. By the time you've reached Colorado, you've spent $3,000, and your cousin in Colorado needs a few hundred to help him get by. Do you leave the money?

Gifting is a personal decision that only you can make, but it is a decision that needs careful consideration and should not be based upon a feeling of guilt or spur of the moment emotion. All of us want only the best for our family. None of us want to be a crutch or negatively influence someone else's life, but the problem with gifting is if you begin the process too soon, you may find yourself in a position where your life is negatively impacted by assets that have left your hands.

We've all seen the phrase on the back of Winnebago's, motor homes, and cars these days where a bumper sticker reads, *"We're Spending Our Children's' Inheritance"*. While many find that cute, there are families that cringe at the mere thought of not having anything passed on to them in the years to come. Call this greed, laziness, or lack of planning, but either way many siblings are counting on Mom and Dad to finance their retirement.

You should never feel obligated to start giving to your children or grandchildren just because you think it would help ease their financial burden. Giving too early can create just as many issues as not giving at all. Your intent may be to help children, grandchildren, church, or local charities, but your giving should be based upon what you can afford to do today.

If you're unsure whether you are able to start the gifting process, the best resource to turn to is your Personal Retirement Road Map. Take a moment to withdraw a percent of your assets from your investments each year. Exclude these assets in your Personal Retirement Road Map and household budget. The feedback you receive should tell you whether you can afford to share your assets with family. In many cases it will simply be too early, but that doesn't mean you can't begin to think about the process.

I've seen many retirees have a desire to give, but aren't comfortable separating themselves from their assets. One recommendation I've made if they are serious about setting funds aside is to create a "gifting account". This account could be a separate account or asset which may be designated for your family, charity, or church. It is an account which would be similar to the way Christmas accounts worked in years past where you could make deposits to an account throughout the year, and at Christmas time, withdraw funds in order to pay for presents at Christmas time, without going into debt. These accounts can be started with as little as you want to begin with and can last forever.

These accounts can be treated as if they are a budgetary item in your household expenses each month. If your Personal Retirement Road Map affirms you could afford to pay yourself $25, $50, $200, or $500 a month into this account to be given away at a future date, then you could begin to think about gifting opportunities in the future, but if things are just too tight don't feel bad. It's important that you ensure your retirement dreams are being reached before you concern yourself with the dreams of others.

Another consideration with gifting is the amount of the gift and the duration. This issue has created problems within many families and charities as the expectations are for the gifts to continue over time. A problem with gifting is that once the process has begun, there is a feeling of dependence that the process and the amount will continue indefinitely over time. There is a sense of expectation from the recipient, and a sense of obligation from the donor.

I recall Christmas and birthdays when my grandparents were alive. While they were working, I always received very nice Christmas presents and lots of presents to open. On my birthday, I would receive cards that contained checks, and I couldn't wait to spend the money, but once they retired from their jobs and the years went by, the number of gifts became smaller, eventually getting to the point where I just received a card for my birthday.

As shallow as this may seem today, this is the way that many recipients of your gifts may react if your gifts don't measure up to the standards to which they've become accustomed. As you consider the process of gifting, be sure to communicate with everyone involved the purpose of your gift and whether it's a one time gift or the beginning of a process. Just like every day, we expect to see the sun rise in the east and set in the west. Once the gifting process begins, expectations are to see the same gift every year, if not more. Keep the harmony within your family by having conversations about your gift to them. Communicate the reasons for your gift

If you don't know if the process will continue in the future, let them know that. Don't provide them with any false hope of what may come in the future. Be clear and direct with regard to your intention.

Many retirees won't have an opportunity to gift their assets to their children during their lifetimes or may not feel comfortable sharing part of their nest. This is personal decision and you should not feel obligated to do begin the process. The premise behind this book has been to secure your dreams in retirement. Your children and grandchildren will have an opportunity to benefit from your gift in years to come, but if you happen to be in the fortunate circumstances where you could make a difference in your children's or grandchildren's lives, the remainder of the chapter is dedicated to issues that you should consider as it relates to the gifting process.

Gifting to Grandchildren

According to a recent survey by AIG, it was estimated that more than 50 percent of grandparents were or planning on providing financial assistance as it related to the higher education of their grandchildren.

This is perhaps the most common practice that retirees consider which serves as a legacy for their grandchildren. It's funny how as parents, while we want the best for our own children, we often snub them by not providing monetary gifts at a time when they perhaps need it the most such as buying their first home, providing for private school tuition, or paying for family trips. Instead, grandparents choose to help grandchildren by starting a savings account, college account, or trust account that can be used towards college expenses, but before you consider this option, it's important you understand all the specifics and tax consequences that may be associated with your gift.

While many grandparents are interested in providing assistance, they may not be interested in not carrying the burden of paying taxes on the gains and income created from such accounts. There are numerous ways that a grandparent can provide monetary assistance to a grandchild and have the assets owned by the grandchild, but there are consequences you should consider before making these gifts.

One of the more popular gifting opportunities is to create Uniform Gift/Transfer to Minors Account. This account allows a grandparent give or transfer up to $12,000 (as of 2007) per grandparent or $24,000 per grandparents per year to a child that is under the age of eighteen or twenty one, depending on the state.

State laws dictate how UGMA accounts may be invested. In most states, life insurance, c.d.'s, or savings accounts are utilized while the UTMA account allows gifts to be invested in various types of investment vehicles such as mutual funds, stocks, bonds, real estate, even artwork. The account is to benefit the minor on record until he reaches the age of majority which is eighteen or twenty one.

One of the major flaws associated with custodial accounts is that when the child reaches the age of majority, eighteen or twenty-one depending on the state, the child now becomes the owner of the account. The child may then do what they wish with the money. You hope they use it towards college expenses, but once they reach the age of majority, it's theirs to do with what they wish.

Another problem with custodial accounts is if a child is receiving financial aid for school, the child's sudden ownership of the account funds could jeopardize his or her eligibility for financial aid for college. College students that have large savings or investment accounts are less likely to qualify for financial scholarships.

Custodial accounts over the years have been problematic for grandparents. Their intentions were to help their grandchildren with funding college expenses, but once they retained full ownership of the account, it was as if they won the lottery. Suddenly they were presented with a large sum of money that they could spend on anything they wanted.

Congress recognized the issues with custodial accounts and in 1996, created an alternative way for parents and grandparents to save for college expenses where they retained ownership of the assets for life. This new plan was called the 529 Plan.

<u>529 Plan</u>

The 529 Plan was named for Section 529 of the Internal Revenue Code, which provides parents, guardians and grandparents an opportunity to set aside funds to be used for qualified educational expenses, whether it's now or in the future. These plans do not have restrictions based upon age. If you have a grandchild who is attending a private school, you could make a contribution to their 529 Plan, and the parents could use these funds to cover tuition, room and board, or other expenses affiliated with the school. If your child is intended on going back to school later in life to advance their degree, you could also make contributions into their 529 Plan as well, regardless of their age.

A unique characteristic of the 529 Plan that makes it different from most custodial accounts is the ownership you have over these funds versus a custodial account. Under the rules of the 529 Plan you as the owner, will oversee how the plan is managed. If the child or grandchild chooses not to attend college, a technical or vocational school in the future, you could name a new eligible beneficiary such as another grandchild, a niece or nephew, a son or daughter, or even the first cousin of the original beneficiary who would be entitled to the funds. If you choose not to name another beneficiary, then assets could be withdrawn from the account and you retain ownership.

Under current law, taxes would need to be paid on the investment gains from the account along with 10 percent penalty. The popularity of 529 Plans not only enables you to remove assets from your estate, but it also provides an opportunity for your grandchildren to pay for educational costs using tax free funds, and if the child chooses not to attend school, you could help another benefactor, or reclaim the assets for other uses.

There are primarily two types of 529 Plans. One type allows you to prepay for the tuition costs in advance while the more popular plan offers the opportunity to invest within state sponsored plans where funds are usually invested in mutual funds to be used for tuition, room board, and other expenses in the future. Under the tax law passed in 2001 the earnings from these accounts are tax-free, but keep in mind this could change this in the future.

Under the guidelines of 529 Plans you are able to contribute up to $12,000 (in 2007) per year ($24,000 for a couple) towards 529 accounts without incurring a gift tax which is 45 percent as of 2007. If you have the means, you could contribute up to $60,000 ($120,000 for a married couple) in the first year of a five-year period, as long as there are no additional gifts to that same beneficiary over the five years, and provide a similar gift in another five year period. In other words, 529 Plans could provide a quick way of getting a sizable amount of money out of your taxable estate (although if you die within the five-year period, the portion of the contribution allocated to the years following your death would be included in your estate).

Because you are the owner of the plan, 529 Plans may not affect a child's eligibility for financial aid. Many universities consider the students income. Custodial accounts will reflect income on the child's tax return but withdrawals from 529 Plans are not considered income to the student. If a child has personal income is too high, it could reduce their chances in acquiring financial aid. Most states now permit or are planning to permit 529 Plans, and many investment firms now offer them as tax—and estate-planning vehicles for their clients. They represent a viable opportunity for you to leave a legacy for your grandchildren to help get them through school. For more information on 529 Plans, consult with your financial advisor or visit www.savingforcollege.com.

If the restrictions involved with Custodial Accounts and 529 Plans make you a bit uneasy, another opportunity to leave your legacy would be to consider a contribution toward tuition costs. Under current law grandparents are allowed to pay the full tuition cost towards of their grandchild's nursery program, private school, or college without incurring a gift tax penalty, only if the payment is made to cover tuition costs only and is made to the provider, school, or college, not the parents, child, or trust.. Other expenses such as room and board, books, and other fees must be paid for through other means. The student may be enrolled full—or part-time, and it's not limited to traditional academic institutions such as colleges and universities. Any educational organization with a regular faculty and curriculum and a student body that meets on a regular basis at a certain place will generally qualify. Just remember, you must pay the school directly.

Many grandparents choose to establish 529 Plans or Custodial Accounts whereby they are able to use their allowable gift donation each year so that their grandchildren have assets set aside for tuition, books, and other fees, and then they write the check to the school or college directly for tuition expenses, thus accomplishing their ultimate goal of providing a full college experience for their grandchild.

If you are looking for a little more control on how the assets you gift to your grandchildren are spent, you could consider a more binding instrument such as a Gift Trust.

Gift Trust

A Gift Trust solves many of the problems gifting money to a grandchild. You will need to consult with an attorney in order to draft a document that expresses your intentions on how assets within the trust are to be used to benefit the grandchild. By using a Gift Trust you can accomplish many tasks with one document:

- Reduce the size of your estate by transferring up to $12,000 (in 2007) into each trust you create for each grandchild. No gift taxes will be due in connection with the transfers;

- Although the trust owns the assets, you control them as trustee and can decide what type of investments to make;

- Income earned by the trust from amounts that you've deposited will not be taxed to you; the trust pays the taxes;
- Amounts deposited in trust, and the income earned from those funds, will be used for the benefit of your grandchildren
- You can provide that the trust terminate at any age you specify.

These trusts are complex legal documents and should not be set up without the help of an experienced attorney. As a result, the chief downside of such trusts is the cost of establishing and maintaining them, which you should discuss with an attorney before going ahead with a trust.

Gifting Strategies for Children, Grandchildren and Charities

A popular investment that has been used by many retirees designed to leave a legacy to their children, grandchildren, church or charity, but still maintain control of their assets has been through the use of annuities.

Over the past twenty years, annuities have become a popular vehicle for investors to set aside money for the future without the worry about additional income tax that could increase taxes on their Social Security benefits. These vehicles have been popular for many years, but carried many restrictions until recently. Depending on who you talk to, you can find someone who will say something good or bad about annuities. If used properly, annuities can offer a great benefit to families and retirees.

Annuities have historically provided an opportunity for investors to save for the future by allowing their assets to grow tax deferred. As discussed in a previous chapter the annuity is actually an insurance contract that has evolved over time and offers numerous features and benefits that aid investors. Today's annuities allow investors an opportunity to invest assets whereby they grow tax deferred, meaning that interest, capital gains, and dividends won't be due from the annuity until funds are actually withdrawn, which if you believe the mathematical studies of compounding, over time means money that you would have sent to the government is earning growing for your benefit.

Annuities allow you to name a beneficiary such as a child or grandchild without relinquishing ownership of the funds. Annuities today even allow the owner of the policy to place restrictions on when the child or grandchild is able to receive the funds and over what period of time. If you find yourself in a position if you don't know for sure if you will need these funds, or you're not comfortable about relinquishing control of your assets, annuities allow you an opportunity to provide a legacy, and remain in control of the assets (subject to potential withdrawal charges, penalties, market fluctuations). After a period of time you feel you don't have use for these assets, you could take distributions from the annuity and provide a gift, transfer the ownership of the policy to a grandchild, or simply leave a legacy by naming the grandchild or child as the beneficiary to receive upon your death.

Annuities have several conditions and restrictions you should consider such as potential tax implications, penalties, management expenses, and early withdrawal fees, but the benefits they provide could provide a lasting legacy that could not only secure your retirement, but the retirement of your child or grandchild.

IRA's

Perhaps one of the best examples you could pass on to your benefactors and decedents are the concept of putting money aside for their own retirement. The life experiences you may have experienced may play some role in this decision, especially if you found yourself in a rush to put money aside for your own retirement. By having a deeper understanding on the pressures of life, you could start the process for your children or grandchildren, and your gift could help them for years to come.

A good option to consider would be to establish a Roth IRA for your child or grandchild. The amounts contributed to such accounts aren't tax deductible, but the earnings accumulated can be withdrawn at age 59 ½ completely tax-free (as long as certain conditions are met). This tax-free compounding can quickly add up, for example, if you have an 18 year old grandchild who has a part time job whereby you could contribute $2,000 to a Roth one time and the investment would be worth $146,000 when they turn 60 (assuming a 10 percent annual return). Also, starting five years after the account has been set up; first-time homebuyers can withdraw up to $10,000 tax-free (under current tax laws).

The Roth IRA could also provide your children with an opportunity to have retirement funds available tax free. The Roth allows the option to choose from several investment vehicles that over time could provide a solid foundation towards their own retirement nest egg.

Don't overlook U.S. Savings Bonds, the most widely held type of security in the world. Savings bonds increase in value monthly and interest is compounded semiannually. Moreover, interest is free from state and local taxes, and federal income tax is deferred until you redeem the bonds. Provided you meet certain eligibility requirements, you can reap special tax benefits if bonds are redeemed to pay for college expenses.

Series EE and the new Series I Bonds make great gifts for grandchildren. Series EE Bonds sell for half their face value. The bond denominations range from $50 to $10,000. If not redeemed when they mature, the bonds will continue to earn interest for up to thirty years. Series I (or Inflation-Indexed) Savings Bonds come in denominations ranging from $50 to $10,000 and are issued at face value. The earnings rate, adjusted semiannually, is a combination of a fixed interest rate at the time of purchase and the rate of inflation. Additional information on U.S. Savings Bonds can be found at the Web site www.savingsbonds.gov Savings bonds can now be ordered directly online

Another product that some retirees have considered is insurance. Many retirees continue to insurance policies which are paid up and carry a cash balance. While some insurance representatives continue to sell life insurance as an investment vehicle, this may not serve your best interest.

At retirement age, the cost to continue to carry insurance and pay for premiums may be cost prohibited. Several studies have pointed out that if assets used to cover premiums for retirees were invested in a growth and income mutual fund, the performance of the fund over the life of the retiree would be significantly higher than the benefit earned.

I'm not going to debate whether life insurance should be considered part of your gifting or estate planning strategy. In some cases it will provide solutions to problems you have in retirement, but these decisions should be based upon how they relate to you reaching your retirement dreams.

IMPORTANT DISCLAIMER:

Remember that gifting should only be considered after many of your dreams have been reached in retirement. Don't ever feel compelled that you need to help your children unless this is part of your Personal Retirement Road Map.

Gifting could open emotional wounds that may never have a chance to heal. Never feel compelled that you need to do something immediately in order to help your children or grandchildren in the future. If you are not comfortable providing some form of gift now, you may make provisions within your will if assets remain in your estate. If you are comfortable in a gifting strategy, make sure that it represents a budgeted item and is part of your Personal Retirement Road Map. While your grandchildren and children should appreciate your gift, they would likely care more of your quality of life and care.

20

Preparing the Next Generation of Retirees

If you were to Google "Baby Boomers Retirement", you would see hundreds of articles explaining whey the Baby Boomer generation is going to have the most difficult time trying to make ends meet in retirement. Many of the stories discuss their lack of saving over the years, their anticipated longevity, medical costs, pension busts, layoffs, and questions about Social Security. It's enough to keep every person who was thinking about retirement in the workforce as long as possible, but some Baby Boomers are going to be fortunate.

Some of you may have had a loved one who provided you with a head start towards your retirement dreams in the form of an inheritance or an IRA where you were named benefactor. If you happen to be one of the lucky individuals who has prepared for retirement, and your Personal Retirement Road Map could tolerate a few more distribution of assets, you should consider passing on your good fortunate to generation X, Y, and Z to come.

Since the introduction of the Individual Retirement Account and pension plans, many Americans have taken advantage of the opportunity to defer payroll dollars and retirement assets within a tax sheltered account to be used for another time. Retirees today have an opportunity to tap into these funds once they reach age 59 ½, but due to their conservative nature to protect their nest egg, many choose not to. There's something about the psyche in knowing that there are funds available to them if they absolutely need them, so they continue to build until at age 70 1/2, the tax laws mandate that they begin to take distributions from these accounts. While some may speculate the reason the government makes us do this is so we could actually enjoy some of the fruits of our labor, the real reason has more to do with potential revenue in the form of income taxes.

If you find yourself in need of the funds, then by all means, use them to pursue your retirement dreams and goals, but if you find that a portion of the distributions from your retirement accounts could be used to begin the nest building process for your heirs, then you may want to consider avenues that could ensure their retirement in years to come.

Some options you can consider in order to begin helping X,Y, and Z, lay the groundwork for their own Personal Retirement Road Map include; irrevocable life insurance trusts, Roth IRA's for children or grandchildren who qualify and have earned income, or annuities which name you as the annuitant and children and grandchildren as the beneficiaries. Taking these steps could go a long way towards securing their retirement future, and educate them on the importance of preparing for the future.

Gifting strategies were discussed in an earlier chapter to help your children, but perhaps the best help you could provide would be in the form of making sure that their retirement dreams and goals have an excellent chance of being reached. The education of grandchildren is important, but so too are the fundamental principles of saving for the future.

Your attorney, tax advisor, or financial advisor should be able to consult with you regarding these opportunities, but these are just a few ideas where you could use funds that could be of great use as they make preparations to build their own nest egg for retirement.

Conclusion

No matter your age or where you may be in your life, mistakes will always be a part of your life. Some mistakes are insignificant while others could cause a great deal of pain or damage. Our experiences could help in the decision making process to avoid similar mistakes in the future, but sometimes you're put into new situations where you can't rely on past experience and a new one is created.

It took me twenty one years before I realized how smart my father was. I can remember several occasions when I challenged his advice and ultimately found myself in an uncomfortable position. Like most kids growing up, I always knew what was best for me. My arrogance and confidence forced me into many decisions that were not good choices. I recall the conversations when my father would tell me that if I listened to him, things would be much easier on me in the future. Well of course I chose a different path. I enrolled in The School of Hard Knocks where my curriculum indoctrinated me in areas where I could hopefully avoid similar mistakes in the future.

As I travel through life, I continue to talk with my children about my life experiences and the lessons I've learned. One of the conversations we have is that I don't have all the answers, and that I will always make mistakes, but when I do, I will do my best to share my experience so they can avoid making similar mistakes.

This is one of the primary reasons I took the time to write this book. I've seen other books that dealt with retirement, but I didn't see any that provided real solutions to problems retirees will face in retirement. This book was written to prepare retirees for their ascension into retirement, it was also meant to serve as a survival handbook you could rely on for answers when you make mistakes or when roadblocks prevent you from moving forward. You will make mistakes that could alter your retirement dreams and goals. Some of these mistakes will be self inflicted because you did not believe, listen, or heed advice. Others will be beyond your control. What is important is not to panic and allow your emotions get the best of you when they occur.

Speak with someone who has climbed Everest and most of the conversation starts with the preparation and the climb to the summit. Very little of the conversation involves the perils faced on the way down. Retirees could face many perils saving for retirement, but there are just as many perils that face them in retirement and they will need real remedies to help them get back on course to their ultimate dreams and goals. While this book can serve as a survival handbook, your Personal Roadmap Road Map will serve as the resource to keep you moving towards your dreams.

I hope that all of you are successful in reaching your summit and just as successful in finding your way back home.

Appendix A

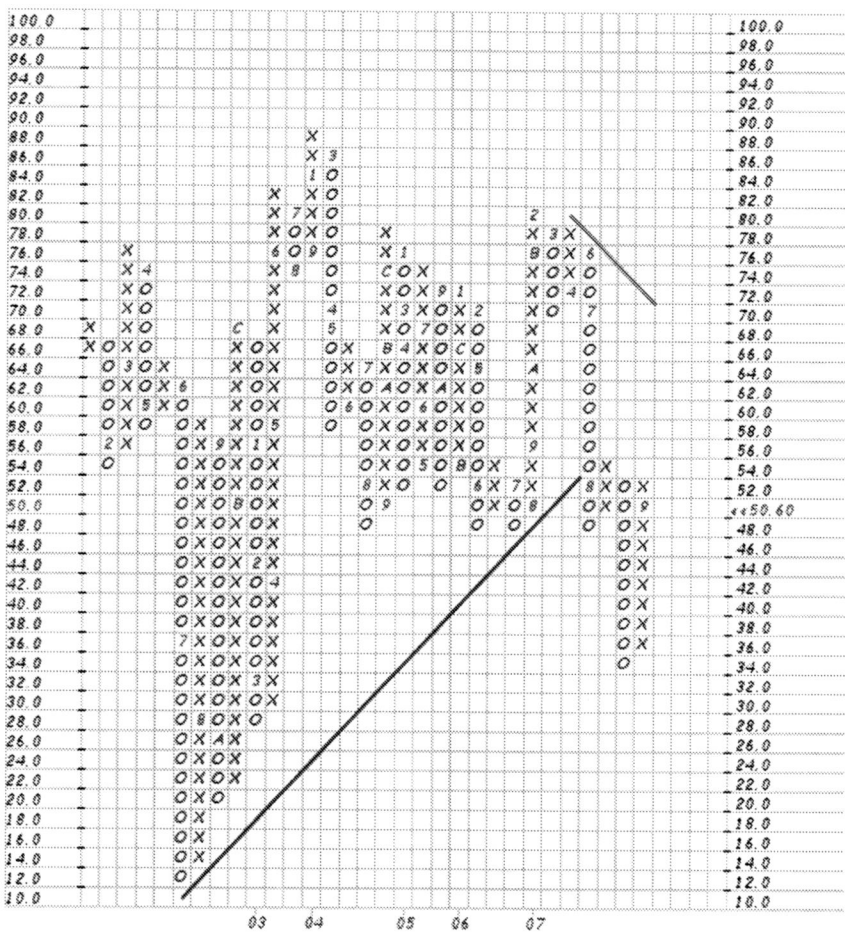

978-0-595-45538-6
0-595-45538-7

LaVergne, TN USA
15 April 2010
179292LV00003B/72/A